The Book of the Highest Good
Volume 1:
The Beginning Experience

By
Joyce McCartney

The Book of the Highest Good: Volume One:
A Beginning Experience, Second Edition

For Peace and Light Association

Copyright © December 21, 2012 by Joyce McCartney

Cover design: Adam Brown

Produced by Positive Options, Inc.

Second Edition:
ISBN: 13 978-0-9897088-1-4

Printed in the United States of America
Second Edition, 2013

Table of Contents

About the Author 1

Preface: How This Book Is Constructed 3

Forward 5

Step One 7
   The dialogue 7
      The beginning begins...............................8
   Several months later, and still sitting
   by the sunny window. 14
      Later the same day.................................21
      The next day after a night's sleep 22
   Message from The Peaceful One 26
   Commentary 31

Step Two..33
   The dialogue...33
      Just a heartbeat later.............................41
   Message from The Peaceful One 46
   Commentary 51

Step Three 53
   The dialogue...53
      A letter to myself: The Gift of First Love 60
   Message from The Peaceful One......................72
   Commentary 76

Step Four 79
   The dialogue...79
   Message from The Peaceful One 89
   Commentary 94

Step Five 96
   The dialogue 96
   Message from The Peaceful One....................106

Note to Dear Reader 113

Highest Good Version of The Lord's Prayer 116

The Long Story 117

Resources and Readings 126
    The lifestyles of the Peaceful and the Patient ... 126

Additional Readings 130
    Forgiveness and Enlightenment:
      An Introduction 132
    Forgiveness and Enlightenment, 3.7.11 136
    Brothers and Sisters of Grace, 9.29.12 144

About the Peace and Light Association 147

Recommended Books and DVDs 149

Recommended Websites 151

About Our Cover and Logo 154

Forward to the Next Book 157
    The Book of the Highest Good, Volume Two:
      Walk to Freedom 157

The Calling Together 161

About the Author

Joyce McCartney is, in many ways, no different than you. Having grown up in a Midwestern family in a strong religious faith, she did not have unusual spiritual experiences as a child or exhibit unusual abilities. Yet, upon achieving midlife and experiencing many of the difficult times that anyone can and do have, she set her mind on the task of finding God.

Using the life and work of Edgar Cayce as her guide, she explored the subtle states of mind that led to the awareness that all humans have two minds, one the Conscious Mind of everyday physical existence and the other the Higher Mind of the soul. Once in contact with the wise Higher Mind, she was taught how to achieve reliable and consistent contact with this Higher Mind and its family, The Great Oneness. And so, it was the Higher Mind spoke to her about the mysteries of the universe and how to find the Presence of God. She became convinced that this great guidance was and should be made available to everyone and wished to find a way to make it so. This book describes that task and the adventures that she uncovered. It is written as a dialogue between herself and the Higher Mind. She explores topics including: the nature of the spirit realm, other dimensions, the human aura, karma, past lives, health and rejuvenation, historical events, the life of Christ, and the plan for restoring peace upon the Earth. Unable to contain all of these topics in one book, she plans a series of books on such topics. Come and join her on the inner adventure of exploring your own Higher Mind and expect to be loved, healed and guided to your own Highest Good.

The Series:

Book of the Highest Good, Vol 1. A Beginning Experience
Book of the Highest Good, Vol 2 Walk to Freedom
Book of the Highest Good, Vol 3 Being of Light
Other Volumes to be announced on PeaceandLight.net.

Preface:
How This Book Is Constructed

This book is about the Highest Good and what it can do for us. In ancient Egypt the Highest Good was symbolized by the ankh symbol and it was used by a peaceful founder to do a lot of good, creating a great society of wealth and peace. After the great Golden Age, the concept was forgotten and then reopened over and over again until the life of Christ portrayed it as peace and brotherly love. Today the Highest Good is still at work making peace, but is not generally written about in simple and direct terms and so I wrote this book in a very conversational style, which anyone can read and understand.

How this material was obtained is described in step one, and the intention was that the highest and best information and guidance be given, not only for myself, but for all who come to read this book. Later, I found that this is, in fact, the definition of the Highest Good; to intend good and nothing else. I was assured that if the intention for the Highest Good were left to play out in time on a large scale, that the same good that took place on the plains of Egypt would also repeat in today's time and place in a new way. As wisdom would have it, it is a journey of personal healing as well as a rebuilding of a great society, thus it is indeed a very personal experience that will replicate on a global scale, maybe even touching your life.

In order to provide many different readers a variety of ways to understand the message of the Highest Good, this book has been written in five steps, each containing a dialogue, a channeled reading and commentary. As you read, you may find that one form is more understandable for you than another. The goal is that the different formats help as many people as possible discover their place in the universe.

The five steps are the traditional stages of opening to Enlightenment as are described in many spiritual texts and were used in the ancient Egyptian Mystery Schools as evidenced by the step pyramids. The five steps, well completed, do in fact lead to an Enlightened State of Being of which there are many degrees and experiences.

Each step offers several tools for the enhancement of the experience. You can choose to use these tools as they seem to work best for you. And so, there is a color, a stone, an herb, a scent, a musical note and a physical/emotional response listed at the beginning of each step. While participating in each step, one might wear the suggested color or use colored paper to write on, have a book on herbs handy to learn about them, drink herb tea or enjoy dried herbs in a vase. One might smell essential oils and play the music that emphasizes certain musical notes to enhance the experience. It could even be as simple as keeping a stone in your pocket or nearby on your table.

As the steps progress, there is a corresponding emotional reaction that will be the guide as to when that step is starting and completing. There is no value to going fast or slow. It's more important that one fully experiences the events of their lives in such a peaceful way so as to receive the most joy and happiness. Be assured that these simple processes influence healing and progress on all levels, including the health of the body. Although I recount the experiences as mine, they are essentially universal, so just relax and experience the joy of finding out the answers to the three great questions of life: Who am I? Why am I here? Where am I going?

Forward

As we move forward on the path of life, there are many occurrences that seem to make no sense. There are happy experiences, but then they are so often followed by sadness. Some are just sad beyond belief. Since I was already deep into one of those really sad events, as well as to make sense of life itself, I decided to try to unravel the whole mess and determine the answers to the great question of life: Why do good and bad things happen to people?

To do this, I took the material that I had at hand to work with: My own situation and thoughts. These seemed like too little to make much out of, but in fact, they turned out to be a great treasure. With these human realities in hand and fully understood, there was not much else that I found to be of any value. Therefore, I have written a tale to share with you of healing and forgiveness, of justice lost and found, of humor enjoyed, of health and wealth regained, and of sadness and grief ended forever.

As a reader, you will have much to say about what you are about to peruse, but let us proceed in peace, for step by step it will all unfold in a way that you do not expect. In time, you will come to see how one wish to be happy came to found a great enterprise of peace and to reopen the secrets of the universe. And so I urge you to stay your judgment until the end. The beginning is sad but the ending is very great and each step along the way is blessed. No need went unfulfilled, no sadness went unrelieved, and no loneliness went unrequited. The power that was contacted was so great that all that was amiss was given a loving finish. The love that was lavished started so small and grew so fast and was so great that the heart burst open, releasing all of its pain, and allowed the body to begin to reshape itself into its original healthful form.

So come along with me, and don't blush to be included in some of the scenes or to be blessed with the grace of a better understanding of your own life experiences. For just as your inner being is made of light, so it lives off of light and does not wish to be sad or homeless in the dark. It can make the grade and come back in a grateful state. So let's continue, or rather start at a beginning much like many beginnings before and since, possibly like yours or mine or many more that are different in some ways, but the same in others.

And so it is with the intention to give you the Highest Good that I start. And with you in such good hands, there is much that will come that is grace itself.

Step One

Color: Purple
Stone: Amethyst
Herb: Goldenrod
Scent: Lemon
Musical Note: C
Physical/Emotional Reaction: Seeking relief of stress

The dialogue

Joyce: We are sitting at a sunny window. You and I are one now as you read this, but at the time of the writing we were separate. In being separate, we warmed up to each other slowly and at first left much unsaid. As the days and weeks progressed, others – who engaged in a dialogue that at once was quite strange but yet inevitable – joined us.

The reason I say inevitable is that I was at the end of all lies and my life was in ruins despite my best efforts. There was nowhere else to go but *somewhere* else. It looked to me like a great abyss of nothingness. But, this time I wanted the truth. You knew it, and I knew it. That's why we met.

It was not just chance or fate. It was quite purposeful. We wanted nothing else than to be together to face the breakdown of one life and the start of a new one together. The pain would have been too great without you to hold my hand as I drove over the cliff of my misery.

Dear Reader, you are the last to join us and we greet you as our lost one at last returned. How could we be whole and happy without you? As you read these pages, I know that you send your compassion and best wishes. For if I succeed, then you do, too. Welcome to my compassion, as I know the defeats and questions that you must feel. Although at first you will not understand what you are about to read, please stand by me. Think about it and wait to understand. For by entering through a different portal of understanding, we can assist each other to find peace. Once we have peace, we will have everything else.

I thank you for coming. I have missed you for so long, and now you are here. So let's begin at the beginning and walk this path together.

+

The beginning begins

It is a beautiful, but discouraging day in March. The sun is streaming in through my window at home and warming me, but I barely feel it. I am worried, sad, and anxious. As I faced the second disastrous divorce of my life, I decided that my life was just not working despite my efforts to make it turn out better. I felt helpless, maybe even incapable. I concluded that before I do any more damage to myself, that it was best to just stay put at home rather than try to make things right. Thus I sit and think in my sunny window.

I think about the past and how I set out as a young person to do the best that I could with my life. I was always an optimistic child and made others uncomfortable with my strange statements of grand designs that I thought I could fulfill. I thought that I could be happy forever. Nothing could stop me from doing what I wanted to do with my life. How innocent I was of what was to happen. When the moment came that my grand designs were denied, the skeptics shouted: "I told you so." It culminated when I was told as a child that life was all about suffering, and indeed I should get used to it. Awash with grief and discouragement, I learned to keep my designs to myself, but Inside I rebelled and thought that it was just too sad to be true.

Being educated in a manner that wished all to have the same beliefs and none to think otherwise, I kept my inner thoughts secret. I learned that not many wanted to hear what I really thought. Worse yet, even I wasn't sure of the nature of my own thoughts. As I grew up, I wanted to be a teacher and a counselor to help others. And since that plan fit into the expected parameters within which I lived, it was accomplished.

Later, I wanted to be happily married and to have a family like the one that I came from. A simple request, but it was not to be, for I never found the perfect mate. What seemed good at first quickly turned sour with deceit, criticism, and resistance. I tried to make it work and exhausted myself in the process. I finally concluded that others were not of the same mind as me. What my mind was about was possibly not something others could even understand or want. I wondered if I were indeed alone. And so, after the children had grown, the first marriage failed, and I wondered what was next and who was next. But, with the second marriage, there were the same issues, just living in different bone and muscle. Two times I've tried and failed, yet seemingly have nowhere to turn to find a better way. I decided that it was time to make a drastic revision of what's going on here.

+

Joyce: So here we sit and think, you and I and Dear Reader, as so many conflicting thoughts roam through my mind. On one hand, I think of the many

9

good things in my life and on the other the sheer meanness that populates human behavior. I have thoughts of anger and fear and occasionally thoughts of peace and happiness. I've lost my way for sure. Which is the truth? Which am I? Why so much confusion? In fact, there seems to be a crowd of thinkers in my mind. I would not care to talk about this to anyone but you.

Other One: What was that last thing that you said? Maybe a crowd of thinkers?

Joyce: I don't know. There just seems to be a confusing jumble of thoughts as if there were strangers in my mind having an argument.

Other One: Why don't you ask each of them what they are thinking?

Joyce: Well, OK, but first of all, who are you?

Other One: You can call me the Peaceful One.

Joyce: Who are the others?

Peaceful One: There is the Fearful One, and then some others who come and go.

Joyce: How about I just deal with the two of you?

Peaceful One: OK, what would you like to ask?

Joyce: How come I am in such a mess? I don't have any work or money. I don't have a car that I can drive anywhere even though I paid for three cars. I am living alone and was deceived and betrayed once again by a relationship. I'm not doing very well with my life! I am a real failure.

Fearful One: I most certainly agree. Look at how poorly you selected your relationships and how you accepted such poor treatment for so long. You should have known better. Your parents would be ashamed of you. Furthermore, I don't see much hope for you in the future. It will take years for you to get through the legal and financial problems that you created and to get back on your feet. Then you are doomed to live a lonely life, for surely no one can love you the way that you expect. Obviously, you can't count on anyone else for support.

Joyce: I wish I could argue with that, but right now, I can't. Why is this all happening to me? What did I do so wrong?

Fearful One: You had a good childhood, but you are too emotional and weak to live in the real world. It is a wonder that you made a living at all. You let everyone walk all over you and you don't speak up for yourself. You should get angry and tell people off.

Joyce: Stop right there, you're making me tired and upset. If I get any more angry, I'll probably have an ulcer. I'm just going to look out this window and relax.

Peaceful One: Have a peaceful day, Beloved One, for you are fine and did not do anything wrong. In fact, you are getting stronger every day and you will get all of the help that you need. Have a nap and rest.

Later:

Joyce: How long have I been sleeping? It must have been for a long time because I feel much better. But, I guess I could be doing something productive.

Peaceful One: Make yourself a good meal and straighten up your room. Also call your sister, as she is worried about you. There is nothing urgent for you to do for quite a while. So relax. Even if you do nothing, all will work out for you.

Joyce: How do you know that? It doesn't look like that to me now.

Peaceful One: Don't you remember who I am? Don't you remember the time that you were little and were lost in a crowd and couldn't find your family? It was I who told you to look up to see the tops of their heads. And then you saw your father and ran to his side.

Joyce: Wow, I hadn't thought of that for a long time. I felt so lost. So just who are you anyway?"

Peaceful One: I am a part of you just as the Fearful One is. I've come to help as I always do when you ask for me. So what would you like to ask of me first?

Joyce: How about going back to work? If I could get a job, I could make some money and get out of the house and maybe make some friends. At least I wouldn't be so lonely, and I could pay my bills.

Peaceful One: That is part of the plan, but not for a while. There are other more important things that you must attend to first.

Joyce: Like what?

Peaceful One: Like, the nap that you took. Do you realize that you relaxed your stomach and your jaw? When you did that, your body could actually function normally. But as you woke up, you started all over again to clench your teeth and strangle your chest and stomach with tension.

Joyce: No, I didn't realize that. I don't even feel my body at all. I can't even tell if I am tense. Anyway, it will all go away if I get back to work and start solving some of these problems.

Fearful One: That's right. No decent person in this society today is unemployed and not actively looking for work. You can't possibly solve any problems by just taking a nap and relaxing. That's so ridiculous. What are you thinking?

Joyce: I just took a nap and felt better, but now I am exhausted again thinking about how ridiculous a nap is. How can I ever succeed if I can't even make some phone calls or get online to look for work? I must be at the worst part of my life. I used to be such a success.

Fearful One: Now you're thinking my way.

Joyce: What?

Commentary

Before I understood that we all have two parts to our minds, I was confused. I wavered between fears and lack of confidence on the one hand and peace and self-esteem on the other. I didn't realize until later how different the two aspects of my mind really were. It was much later when I realized that I was choosing to be in agreement with the Fearful One by judging and criticizing myself and would get nothing but grief in return. On the other hand, I could agree with the Peaceful One by being positive and get all kinds of help. The Peaceful One was helping me, and the Fearful One was causing me harm, tension, anxiety and later even illness. Now I see this much more clearly.

+

Dear Reader, I know that you may not have heard from the Peaceful One and Fearful One in the manner that I describe, but would you admit to having such thoughts as these? Perhaps the Fearful One is like a constant companion, while the Peaceful One is a rare visitor. Would you admit to having had some of these same life experiences or ones equally confusing? Perhaps that is why we are now here together. Maybe we can be of help to each other.

+

Several months later, and still sitting by the sunny window.

Joyce: Why do I not see anything getting any better? It's been months, and things seem to be the same or even worse. I do a little something each day to help, but it doesn't have much effect. What am I doing wrong?

Fearful One: Don't ask me. You are responsible for your condition, and no one can figure this out but you. You obviously can't get anything right. If it's not working by now, then it never will.

Joyce: Now, wait a minute. I tried being angry, and it was a disaster. It caused me a big setback. That is clearly not going to help me. There must be something better. Sigh. **I just want to be happy**.

Peaceful One: Welcome, dear one. You have spoken very powerful words in asking to be happy. That's what we want for you, too. You can be happier right this very moment. How's the sunny window today?

Joyce: Actually, quite nice. The seasons are changing, and I'm watching the leaves grow on the trees. I even put out my bird feeder and watched the tiny birds come and go.

Peaceful One: You are much like those birds. They are innocent and have no worries, for all that they need is supplied to them by nature. The same is true for you. Do you remember the story that Jesus told about the birds of the field?

Joyce: I love that story. It reminds me of happy summer days in the country. I love the thought of Jesus telling the story to comfort the crowds. Well, I do have food and water and a roof over my head for now, but not much more. It is peaceful here, and nobody bothers me. I do get bored, though.

Peaceful One: Why don't you read one of your inspiring books on the bookshelf?

Joyce: Ok, let's see what I have. Here's my favorite book on Edgar Cayce and his readings. He obviously helped a lot of people and had quite a following. Maybe he can help me. What did he mean by "As above, so below?"

Peaceful One: Cayce was talking from the place of his Higher Mind, incorporating all of the wisdom, grace, and healing energy of the light that resides there. The people who came to him for readings were residing in their Conscious (or lower) Minds and could not understand the Higher Mind very well. Throughout his life, he lent them a glimpse of the potential of their Higher Minds by saying that the Higher Mind gives good, but the Conscious Mind sees fear and conflict.

As above, so below and not vice versa. Your pain exists only in your Conscious Mind, not above in your Higher Mind from which we are speaking.

Joyce: I thought so! There is something real about the conversations with the two parts of my mind that I've been having, isn't there?

Peaceful One: Yes, indeed, and there is much to learn about the two. Actually, there is no difference between the two but a little time and space. Most importantly, there is no need of a barrier between us.

Only doubt and fear separate us. You can trust the Highest Good that we send to you.

Joyce: So you said that your place has light in it and only wants good, right? What do you mean by the light?

Peaceful One: Light is life in motion, freely and constantly giving all good things. It originates from the Source of all Creation and is still burning brightly everywhere in the universe. The light of the sun is an example of it, but ironically, also the spark of life in a blind cricket living deep within a cave. In fact, all physical reality is made from light, including you. The above place where we reside has been called by many names. Jesus referred to it as his Father's Home. And as with all good fathers, it is the source of much life, love and goodness, which can manifest into your physical realm.

Joyce: You said the magic word: Manifest. Why aren't things going better for me yet? Things just don't work out for me. I'm cursed to always have bad relationships. I just know it.

Fearful One: I'll say! Let's review your love life and see that you have never been really accepted and loved. You've always been a strange one, and no one really understands or accepts you. Worst of all, you only faked being happy.

Joyce: OK, maybe you're right. I never am truly happy. Maybe no one is ever really happy. I guess we just get old and die.

Fearful One: That's the way it's always been. No reason that it won't happen to you as well.

Joyce: Thanks for that happy thought! So what about Cayce's healings and the life of Christ? Cayce helped people, and Christ promised resurrection and eternal life. What's that all about?

Peaceful One: I'm glad you asked. Cayce helped a lot of people by giving healing remedies to those in need. Christ went through the same fears that you are having and came out the other side still alive and in even better form. You will too, but you don't have to die to find out.

Joyce: Is that what this is all about? Fear?

Peaceful One: The only one fearful is the Fearful One. Fear exists only in the fearful part of one's mind and nowhere else. The rest of the natural world is happy – just as you will be. That is what the birds at the feeder experience. All is made of light and is good, except fear.

Joyce: What?

+

Commentary

Dear Reader, I know that this part about the two minds is possibly confusing, but I took a closer look at the Fearful One and saw that it was true. The fears that I thought about were from experiences in my life and had acquired great power in my thinking. They expanded as I thought about them, feeding me more discouraging thoughts and even manifesting bad events in my life, so that more fearful experiences only proved their viability over and over. The longer I paid attention to the fears, the worse they became.

On the other hand, clearly, the Peaceful One was helping me and more importantly, I felt loved. The more I thought about The Peaceful One, the more good and loving things came to be. I still couldn't believe that they were both part of me, but I was the only one sitting in the sunny window, except now, you, Dear Reader. That makes two of us, unless you, like myself, also have a Fearful One and a Peaceful One. That would make six of us. How confusing is that?

However, I sensed that I could choose which aspect of mind to listen to, and I wanted more of the Peaceful One and less of the Fearful One for sure. I hope that you agree with me, for it proved to be a fateful decision for me and will be for you as well.

As soon as I made that decision, I found that at first the fears were even harder to deal with because they had so much evidence to support them and I had a long habit of thinking about them over and over again. I was literally feeding them and they were growing into monsters. It would be hard to break that habit. How could I believe in good, when there were so many examples of pain and suffering, not only in my life, but in all of society. I had to stop watching TV. It was too painful to see and hear of the suffering of others and know that it was fear at work.

Finally, I realized that fears were so prevalent in our society because people paid attention to them and excluded the peaceful, good parts of their minds in skepticism and discouragement. I'd hate to think that all of history was a reflection of the same attention to fear. The good news is that whatever we pay attention to will manifest, the bad news is that it includes fears.

All of the sudden, it hit me like a ton of bricks that I'd better get control of what I think about and sort them into two categories: Fear and Peace and chose which to invest in. If I didn't, then fears would manifest in my life and, in fact, in the general society to such an extent that they would become reality for us all. Everybody would accept them as fact because they experienced them. But they will not realize that the fearful events originated with fearful thoughts. This was a horrible, but freeing, realization.

The thing that kept me going, indeed, was that I wanted better things from the Peaceful One, not only for myself, but for all of us. I liked the phrase "Trust the Highest Good." I wanted and needed a lot of good, so I wrote it on a small slip of paper and placed it in the hand of my favorite angel statue. Although she was only made of porcelain, she seemed to be holding it up for me to see whenever I felt fearful. It was very helpful, especially because progress was very slow. I concluded that although good was on the way, it took a long time to show up as a manifestation.

Dear Reader, if you have ever whispered a prayer, would you do so now and help us both? Ask to avoid the fearful thoughts and stand open to the Peaceful One. It will help me and possibly save you from much pain and suffering. It may help your loved ones avoid it as well. It would be a comfort to both of us that we contributed to peace rather than to fear.

If we are to proceed, I have to find out more. Let's ask more questions.

+

Later the same day.

Joyce: Can we pick up where we left off? If you are helping me, how come things aren't getting better?

Peaceful One: You are sleeping better aren't you? Doesn't your stomach feel better? Aren't you just a little bit happier when you watch the birds?

Joyce: Well, yes, but that has no effect on my big problems. I'm beginning to doubt that you will be of any real help. It's just like praying and nothing ever happens. It's kind of a cruel trick that they play on children who don't know any better; to get hopes up and then never produce results.

Fearful One: That's right. There is no Big Daddy in the sky wanting to help you. Just look at you now. Time is going by, and you've not accomplished anything. Time to take things into your own hands. You could go to the drug store and get some pills that would help you sleep better or settle your stomach in no time. You've been at this same point for months and do the same thing every day. Worse yet, you are running out of money, and the legal process has you on delay for many more months. Nothing good has happened at all.

Joyce: I must be a fool to have believed the Peaceful One. It's getting me nowhere. I'm so sick and tired I can hardly think about anything any more. I feel dizzy and nauseous. I'm going to bed.

The next day after a night's sleep

I sent a pleading glimpse at the porcelain angel holding the little note I placed in her hand as I brushed my teeth. Then I sat down to talk to the Peaceful One.

Joyce: I see another new day with a beautiful sunrise accompanied by birds singing. I am once again wishing that I could be happy.

Peaceful One: Look at the sunrise and notice the colors changing as the sun ascends. Listen to the birds a little longer. It refreshes your mind and heart.

Joyce: Yes, I'll worry about my problems later. I think I'll take a walk.

Peaceful One: Notice the warm sun on your face and the sweet, wet grassy smell in the air. Which direction would you like to go? Go wherever you like. You are free to be happy right now.

Joyce: I like this, and I don't feel tired. I think when I get back that I'll check my e-mail. Maybe there'll be some good news.

Peaceful One: Only good things will come to you. No harm and lots of good. We call this the Highest Good.

Joyce: The walk was wonderful, and I feel so refreshed. I'll check my messages. E-mail looks about the same. But there is a call from a friend who needs some help. I'll get that done first. It'll be fun to help him out.

Later, after the phone conversation:

Peaceful One: You have done a good thing. You must be capable of good, don't you think?

Joyce: Well, if you put it that way, yes. If I can *do* good, then I must *be* good. I was wondering, if you don't mind answering another question, does it help if people think positive thoughts? I mean, like if I imagine me working, would that make it happen?

Peaceful One: Try it and see

Joyce: Well, I have been imagining myself working for quite a while now and nothing has happened. Exactly how long does it take?

Peaceful One: As long as it needs to. Did it make you feel good?

Joyce: No, not really. If it doesn't happen right away, I get discouraged and begin to doubt everything – including you. It made me tired.

Peaceful One: Well, then stop imaging it. Just trust that it will come eventually and forget it. Trust in your Highest Good and it will be done for you.

Joyce: What does Highest Good mean?

Peaceful One: It means that as you come to know that you are made from goodness and that goodness is what you are all about, that it will show up in your daily experiences. In addition, what is good for you is also good for everyone else, and no harm will come to anyone who asks for it.

Joyce: But what if good doesn't come? What will happen to me then?

Peaceful One: Why not set the intention for yourself that you are good and that only good can come for you whether it is a job or something else? By the way, you don't have to constantly search your mind for fears and stamp them out like forest fires. Set your intention for having only the Highest Good and all else will be taken care of.

Joyce: What? Can I do that? It sounds so easy. Will it work?

+

Commentary

Dear Reader, I am so glad that you are still here. I need lots of support on this point. I could slowly see that I was spending less time listening to the Fearful One and that I felt better. Getting upset was certainly not helpful. But how much could I do by just trusting the Highest Good?

I didn't get the full answer at this time, but later I came to realize that since the Peaceful One had only good to give – and if I aligned my intentions and thoughts to that – that I was helping to bring good things to myself with great power and grace. I just didn't know what or when. It came in very small steps, and it only gradually increased.

Actually, as I later found out, I needed only to open my mind to *letting* good happen. The great value in refusing to listen to the Fearful One is that it left my mind *open* for something good. It kept me peaceful and not so tired. By not spending time and energy on being fearful and causing setbacks, I could attend to much better things.

But I had to choose it for myself. If I got negative or doubtful, the Peaceful One would vanish instantly and the Fearful One would reappear. I was learning a lot, but it was a start-and-stop kind of thing: one step forward and two back, so to speak. No wonder things did not manifest very quickly for me. I repeated "Trust the Highest Good" over and over again – even if it did not seem to be working.

Dear Reader, we've taken the first step together to avoid the Fearful One thriving in our minds. It seems like a huge task, but actually, we don't have to think that we need to fix all of our problems or even understand them. It's much more simple than that. Just ignore the fears and get interested in the Peaceful One. It's a much better way to live because you get to skip the pain and just get on with the good. When I opened my mind to that possibility, I discovered that the Peaceful One found a way to heal the Fearful One without me knowing how, so that it, too, eventually became happy and we could live as one. But that is part of the rest of the story.

Message from The Peaceful One

Trusting the Highest Good, 12.5.12

Peace and Light Association
Peaceandlight01@aol.com
PeaceandLight.net

How good a manager of anything can the Highest Good be? That is the question of this reading. For anything to be managed, it needs to be free to be moved around and therefore we come to the necessary precursor of management: Trust. If an employee did not trust that he or she would be directed in a good direction and be paid, he or she would not be employed with that manager. Therefore, the building of trust in the guidance of the Highest Good as presented by The Peaceful One needs to be in existence before anything else can be delivered. In fact, does not this one often reflect upon the many good things that have happened to her since the divorcing of herself from the disrespect of a poor partner, finding that all has been good and getting better each day? With this, we have the need to show how this is happening.

Things happen to each person each day in great multitude and in advance of either fear or love or a mixture of both. "Why, oh why, has this happened to me?" one might ask. No matter what has happened, the answer is sure to be the same, for both outcomes derive from the same source. One is the happy version and the other is sad. The choice of the path of the sad verses that of the happy is solely the property of the free will of the participant. However, even the bad will lead to the good when one decides that it can and should. It might be said that there is no alternative to the Highest Good. Relaxing into the guidance function of being a listener of one's own peaceful mind leading to happiness is the best option.

For this option to be seen as prodigious, it is necessary for one or more of the following to be well understood. There is nothing better to entertain the mind of one in love with oneself than to find the little joys of life. Just like a Japanese paper lantern hanger, the Highest Good has surrounded each with a kind and peaceful garden of delights in which to live while more is in the preparation. Just taking the kindness and joys of a day's encounter in the garden of delights has much to do with propelling one forward to a desired outcome, and is as effective as any spiritual discipline, prayer or religious practice.

With that being said, there are many ways to entertain the mind and to give the grief-ridden heart nourishment. Looking carefully at each event to find a little bit more joy is very benign. Only the disappointment that the biggest and greatest of joys has not yet been offered can stop the flow of good. And even in the event of disappointment, if enough good things have been amassed, then the bad will be counter balanced by the evidence of so much that is good.

Certainly, love is love wherever it is found, and it feeds the heart whatever it can through the thin straw of frail faith in the Highest Good. As the straw opens wider and wider, the fulfillment of joy becomes more and more possible. With that, the good expands. Thus the real issue is not to be given the final gift well in advance of when it can be appreciated, but to open the heart well in advance of the arrival of the gift.

Once early childhood experiences or even later ones have closed one's heart, there is nowhere to go to find anything of much good, for the life energy in the form of joy flows through the heart, or not. If it is closed, then there is a backflow causing much congestion, reflux, and discomfort. Better to declare the heart to be open for loving business all of the time by calling upon the sacred name of God to be our loving guide and giver of all good things. For God to be known directly, is a great gift and is preceded by asking for the Highest Good. It means only that no harm could come from such a fine Source and only good will follow. Thus, it can be trusted – for we have all always trusted our complete existence to it.

For the heart to be open to all of the little goods as well as the big goods, it needs to have free-flowing channels of access. Much like a phone line giving digital impulses, the capacity of the line has everything to do with the transmission. If the line is a thin, frail one, it transmits very little and very slowly. If it is robust and open for more flow, then all manner of good things can be sent and received. Thus we find that the reading on the robust heart is a good one, so let's proceed with that.

A robust heart is one that has known itself to be a receptacle of good and nothing else. For one living in the physical world who has experienced harm and abuse, there is little to persuade the heart to open further for more. Thus it remains open for only a select few experiences, and even those go sour at times. However, a robust heart, even if it has had some abuse, goes purposely to the highest of intentions and slaps a label upon it, saying: "Open only to the Highest Good. None else need apply." With this protection, it is open for more experiences and compassion. With this type of approach, the heart can hold steady and strong in the storms of life, so to speak.

And so the vast quantity of experiences of life available to everyone such as the sun, stars, water, and air – being benign – should be considered at first as a universal starting point. In fact, all of nature is a good place, for no one finds harm in a babbling brook, a sunny field of flowers or a dusty pink sky at sunset. With those harmless experiences firmly in place, there are the joys of living animals and vegetation to consider. For if one had the intention for no harm, one would live like the plants and animals do in complete freedom to be themselves, knowing no fear. Fortune of the financial and social kind would be much the same under the reign of the Highest Good, as such activities would occur with no harm and produce much good both for the giver and the receiver. Many more people would inevitably prosper so well as to create a lifestyle of peace and comfort.

But how likely is it that the Highest Good intention could manifest a love life of grace without harm and giving much grace? Should the human species or more specifically, one of the opposite gender be considered the most dangerous animal on the planet, it would seem that so it would be. But if one has the intention of no harm and much good, then the first-class lovers of good should appear with no intention of remise. For if they should bring an intention for harm, they would be immediately repulsed in fear of receiving so much good that they would have to change their ways. And thus it is so for many.

For many come and stay awhile while many go their ways in peace, and others in disgrace. But the lover of the grace of God's Presence has nothing to fear – for no fear can find a place to rest in such a Presence, and so much that is good cannot help but force the fear to retreat. Thus it has come to pass, that many might meet a being of grace and are caused to sample the Highest Good. Such that stand for good are allowed to stay for the keeping, and one must let the others pass. Often, in finding the keepers, the weeping for joy is too grand a thing to let them go. And thus eventually some may marry and stay together for life.

Such a life of grace is never far away, but for the sake of learning of the ways of grace to exist in a partially opened heart, let us describe what is called the Great Wish experience. Once one has opened one's heart to yet another experience of good, there is always one wish that is so great that it expands the heart. Thus, when the student is ready, the teacher appears. For those who wish the greatest of healings, a completely whole and intact body of light experience, they can chose to experience the step-by-step removal of their fears through the achievement of their Greatest Wish. Should the Great Wish be a relationship, the relationship may start and then pause while each gives thought and consideration. Each time the relationship is approached; fears arise, which require a new and deeper decision to have the wish in a fearless manner. This releases the fear and grief possibly experienced in other relationships. Thus, those who wish to be part of this experience seem to know the exact times to come and then to go for a while. For they are in complete cooperation with each other, each receiving their own releases of fear and grief until both arrive at the precise time to be joined, whole and intact, so totally free from grief that nothing but good can come to them evermore.

Much more can be said, so let us continue with the dialogues. For more good is available to those who have a heart big enough to hold it. So approach this next section with a wide-open heart and a desire to have your biggest wish ever.

Commentary

It was a big step for me as it was for you too, I know, but now that we have looked history squarely in the face, the discovery of the nature of our own mind is the first and most important step to being happy. As soon as one realizes that there are different types of thought experiences that one can choose, then the question is which one is the best. "I think, therefore I am," means that what I think becomes my experience. Then the experience creates your definition of yourself. You are what you choose think and act upon. Because a mind is capable of creating one's experience, one who chooses to dwell in fear will experience fear just like paying to go to a horror movie. But if one can gain the wisdom and discipline to avoid fear and choose more positive thoughts, then the life experience begins to reflect more positive outcomes. One must accept that the progress is slow in the beginning and only later picks up momentum. There are advances and setbacks as the pain and fear are released from the heart.

After a while, the positive becomes so prominent and the fear so distant that the choice stabilizes and allows the person to fully believe that he or she is blessed and that good happens to him or her all of the time.

Far from being just a lesson in positive thinking, it is a turning to the Higher Mind for guidance where peace is the resident emotion and turning away from the fear and sorrow temporarily residing in the Conscious Mind.

And now for the best news of all: I thought about you, Dear Reader, and asked the Peaceful One for a gift to give you to further understand the difference between the Higher Mind and the Conscious Mind, so turn to the end of the Step Five, after the Prayer of the Our Father and read the short article called "The Long Story." It will describe how anyone can get a message from his or her own Higher Mind. Remember that you may only have a faint and very subtle message at first and that it may appear briefly and then vanish when you look for it. It might be an image in your imagination or a song or a feeling on your skin. Be open to whatever you sense, and be grateful. Then ask for it to be strengthened so that it is easier for you to enjoy. Come back after you have read it. I will be waiting for you.

Did you like The Long Story? I hope that it worked for you. The Peaceful One assured me that anyone who honestly tried would succeed, even if just a little. With that started and now that you have returned, you will recall that in Step One, I, Joyce, wanted relief from my stress and grief and said to myself: "I just want to be happy." I hope you did the same. This represents a great turning point for both of us and then much more happens. Eventually Step Two begins.

Step Two

Color: Sage Green
Stone: Ruby
Herb: Lemongrass
Scent: Orange
Musical Note: D
Physical/Emotional Response: Deep Breaths

The dialogue

Almost nine months have passed since I first started this dialogue, and I am still sitting in the sunny window, essentially doing nothing. However, I'm starting to see *some* things changing. I am less fearful, which is helping my health to improve. I can now draw a deep breath without tightness and pain in my chest. I have started the habit of only speaking to the Peaceful One. I use a respectful and loving form of address because I feel so loved. I look at the conversation each day as a necessity. I wouldn't miss it for anything. It gives me great comfort and provides much good company. So let's pick up where we left off.

Joyce: Dear Peaceful One, I welcome you today and am willing to work with you to make my life a happy one. What do you have for me to work on today?

Peaceful One: Let's find some play to do today. What do you enjoy doing, and why don't you do it more?

Joyce: Well, I like to do creative things or take walks. I like sewing and cooking. Why?

33

Peaceful One: The reason that you like these things is that you are living in a physical world and need to express who you really are. For example, if you make something beautiful out of cloth, paper and paint or drawing materials, you are giving your attention to doing so and using your creativity to make beauty. You are a beautiful being doing beautiful things.

Joyce: OK, I think I know where you are going with this. You are saying that I am beautiful and when I make beautiful things, I show a little bit of myself – and that gives me confidence. How am I doing, teach?

Peaceful One: How well you have opened to the grace of being happy! What could you do today to express yourself as a Happy and Beautiful One? If you could know that about yourself for sure, then more happy and beautiful things would show up in your life. Your heart would be more open to being happy, so happiness would manifest in your life.

Joyce: That seems strange to me. Making something beautiful is such a small thing. You are saying that it will manifest as good things in my life. I don't get it. Please explain more.

Peaceful One: Please realize that you are always manifesting because you are a manifesting being. Didn't you notice not long ago that as long as you entered into fears that they showed up in your life – and, in fact, this is reflected in the whole society as well? Investing in fear creates the reality of fear. Why wouldn't it work the other way as well? Just try it and see.

Joyce: You have such a wise way of leading me in the right direction. OK, I'll get busy and see what happens.

+

I went to my box of fabric scraps and found some colors and patterns that I liked. I decided to cut them into small squares and laid them out into a simple pattern, much like a quilt, but just one small square. I began to sew. Later as I looked at my small work of creativity, I felt good about it. The colors and patterns looked happy.

+

Peaceful One: How are you feeling about this experience?

Joyce: Pretty good. It's not perfect. But it was fun, and I learned a lot. I noticed that at one point I almost gave up because I thought that it wouldn't work out. I heard the Fearful One arrive at once and tell me that I had no creativity and was just making a mess. I had to laugh. It's so predictable! Once I give the fears some attention, they come rushing in and make it real if I let them. It was challenging to turn it around. Actually, it caused me such a setback that the project took twice as long.

Peaceful One: If you had let the Fearful One run your life, you would have had a lot of setbacks (called karma). Many people cycle through such setbacks for a long time, even many lifetimes. But since they don't go anywhere good and all beings want good, they inevitably are led back to the good. The important thing is that you are the manifestor and can choose which type of manifestation you want.

Joyce: Wait a minute. Hold the phone. You mean to say to me that all of the bad things that I experienced in my life were manifestations of fears? Are you including my two marriages?

Peaceful One: Yes and no. At first, they seemed good or you would not have entered into them. But then they changed due to the fear of both parties opening up to the fullness of happiness. Finally, one or the other opted out and retreated into their Fearful One. The light of love became hidden.

Joyce: I think I know the very moment that it happened. I felt a cold shiver in my heart. After that, there was no end to the meanness. I've felt this same feeling from so many people all of my life. It is so sad.

Peaceful One: Indeed sad. It takes great courage to try to love another, to keep one's heart open for good and to resist fear. But it is not just relationships. All of your experiences reflect this truth.

Joyce: So by that do you mean that all of the bad experiences of my life came from my fears in my mind? Some people say that it was good for me because it made me stronger.

Peaceful One: What would be the point of saying that good is good and then portraying bad as good? Is not good, truly good. Remember when Christ talked about a loving parent giving their children good things to eat, not a stone?

Joyce: If good is good as you say, then why *do* people say that they got good things from bad experiences?

Peaceful One: If bad experiences come to pass as a result of painful thinking, then there is indeed the opportunity to consider the choice and its outcome and to possibly choose another way. Thus there is the experience that one can find good in everything, including the bad. Such a conundrum is part of living on the physical plane and it was planned that way, so that a path toward good would be laid out that was failsafe, so to speak. But that is not the preferred way. It is much better to choose to live under the protection of the Highest Good and to have lives of service to one's fellow man. With that intention, one can expect good things in all situations without regard to one's own or anyone else's fears.

Joyce: What about blame or fault? Who was at fault?

Peaceful One: Blame and fault are both fearful things to consider – because if one is to blame, then they must be bad, and that means that they are separated from the good. So just for the moment, let's say that there is no such thing as blame or fault except in the thoughts of the Fearful One. How does that make you feel?

Joyce: I can hardly believe it: No fault! Well, it lets me breathe easier, because I did want for both of us to be happy. I didn't want the relationships to fail. It is sad when a relationship could be so good. So why would a couple not take happiness when it is possible for them?

Peaceful One: Perhaps they failed to recognize the Fearful One in themselves and had no access to their Peaceful One. A person can only be as happy as their access to peace will allow them. They may have had only a thin straw to let in happiness. After that straw gave out, the door slammed closed. The choice to avoid fear and to choose peace is the only choice you really have in life and it takes much determination to accept nothing less.

Joyce: Let me think about that for a while. This is one of those things that sounds so right, but is so contrary to the way I always thought and indeed the way everybody else thinks. But in a strange way, it changes everything.

Peaceful One: How right you are. This is the peace that Christ came to give you. It was His version of peace that would last forever without fail. Take your time and think about it. And by the way, keep breathing deeply. It is helping you to release the toxins of fear and draws in life-giving oxygen.

Joyce: Sigh. OK, now I've got a really tough question for you. What about other people who suffer horrible, bad things? Are they all doing the same thing, living in fear?

Peaceful One: Yes and no. You have seen the truth that you and all humans are capable of manifesting both fear and happiness and are entirely free to choose which you want at every moment in time. However, there are those who came to experience some apparently bad things just to lead others to their truth. Look at Christ. He appeared to suffer what he did just to lead you to this moment of truth. He came to show you the way to the Truth of Peace. That is a great gift, don't you think?

Joyce: What do you mean he *appeared* to suffer? By all accounts, he certainly *did* suffer.

Peaceful One: If he suffered in peace, then the suffering was not real for him. In short, he took the blows to provide a sure passage through fear and arrive on the other side intact and safe. He proved it by resurrecting in an even better light body and continuing to teach and heal just as he started out to do. He showed the way even in the worst of conditions, to be at peace. In peace, he had all of the support, good things and healing available from the Great Oneness. We literally healed him as fast as they could destroy him and they wondered what was going on. He died because he chose to and He did so in peace. The same is true for you and your loved ones. Remember when he left, he said: "My peace I give to you. Go in peace." Do you understand now what he meant?

Joyce: Yes, I think that I got it. It all makes sense. He refused to experience fear and ended up in better shape than before because he could access his Higher Mind. The Higher Mind could then provide all life energy and guidance necessary. He wanted me to see that I can do the same. If I choose to invest my attention in peace, love and good things, then my life will change to show the good — and then I will be happy. Even if something bad comes along, if I stay in peace, it will have no effect. Have I got it right?

Peaceful One: Much more than you can know. Yes, you have it right. Do you know why you are writing this book? Is it possible that you are doing what Christ asked you to do? Remember the story where he asked his followers to go and find his lost sheep and to feed them, taking care to lead them into green pastures as He did?

Joyce: What? Are you talking about me?

+

This was a heart-stopping moment in my life. I had been blaming myself for all of my problems, and it never occurred to me that there might be something good that I was trying to accomplish. I knew that I was a good person, but bad things had happened to me. Was there a purpose beyond the stupidity of fearful people treating each other badly over and over again? Was there more to life than that? I had to know.

Dear Reader, I don't mean to imply that you are a lost sheep as I don't know anything about taking care of sheep. But I do know that they like to stay together in flocks and do not venture out on their own for fear of predators. I do not want you to live in fear for I have seen its misery. You are so beautiful that you do not need any suffering due to your own fears. Since I don't know your exact needs, I will just ask that you find greener pastures while I share what I have learned. Would you do the same for me? If so, then we can proceed in safety for we were two and now we are one because we want the same thing for each other and all others.

+

Just a heartbeat later.

Peaceful One: I am listening to your breathing and heart beat change. Your body is reflecting your thoughts, so I supported it with life energy and healed it with grace. Yes, indeed, Beloved One, you have come through these difficult experiences to be here at this moment talking to me and sharing it with the reader. And the reader has come through many experiences as well to be here with us and to help their loved ones. Our purpose is all the same. We are one great family, and we help each other.

Joyce: I am breathless, indeed. Do you mean to say that I did not screw up? That I had a good purpose? That the purpose was to write this book and to help others?

Peaceful One: Yes, I do mean that. You intended just this when you started this long journey, and I agreed to be here with you helping – as did all of the other people in your life. Don't you see what a great being you are and how many other great beings are present with you to support you?

Joyce: OK, now you have me on fire with questions. What about the one who hurt me so much? Was that person here with me for a good purpose?

41

Peaceful One: You named this person the Mean One. How about you use the name Fearful-Angry One. It will make it easier for you to understand your relationship.

Joyce: Oh, I see! Now I get it. The Fearful Ones are mean because they bought into their fears and manifested so much pain in their lives that they became angry, thinking that being miserable was their fate so they wanted company. They believed that fear was fact, so it was OK with them to hurt other people. And I came into that experience to show another way. No wonder I felt so hurt, I was feeling his lifetime of hurt and anger and then took it as my own.

Peaceful One: Keep going. You are glowing so bright and happy at this moment. Your beauty and grace are starting to be more evident to you.

Joyce: Well, I don't know where to go from here. This changes everything. It means that I am good and have a good purpose and that there are only Fearful Ones to fear. OK, now let's stop there. Could a Fearful One actually hurt me? What good would that be? Why would I sign up for pain and harm just to prove a point to someone else?

Peaceful One: Oh, how far you have come. You are a blessing upon this Earth, which wishes to be happy as well. No, no one can actually harm another unless both buy into the fear. If one chooses not to be in fear, the situation instantly changes into escape from supposed harm. Perhaps you have heard of people who were threatened and somehow managed to escape or survive. They tell inspiring stories. Yours is one of them.

Joyce: Stop right there, I can also think of exceptions to that line of thought. What about innocent babies and children who are harmed and even die when they have no choice in the matter.

Peaceful One: Their choice is to be there for a short time or maybe not and to move back into spirit form without pain whenever they wish. This type of choice is at the soul level, not the conscious one. This is especially true for the innocent ones, who have not yet developed a Conscious Mind.

Joyce: This is hard to understand. Help me out here.

+

Are you struggling as much as I am with this part? As you do, notice how the topics are leading to a higher understanding of how big and powerful we are, you and I. At once a conundrum that can't be answered by the ordinary ways of understanding reality, it opens to great truths if you ask for a higher understanding.

I invite you to open our joint mind to the possibility that we are both beautiful souls of spirit form as well as humans living in a physical body; Me typing at a computer creating this book and you reading it. In the Higher Mind we are one. We always were and always will be. In the belief of fear, or we shall call it the Conscious Mind, we seem to be two separate ones. Gratefully we have avoided being mean to each other just to defend our shaky view of ourselves. If we had not avoided being mean, we would have had to play a game of: "Can you hear me now?" In this game, one is mean to another who then has to chose to be mean back or to hear with the Peaceful One or Higher Mind where they are at peace and respond with help and peace. Have you ever played that game and still gotten meanness back? Me, too, and its not much fun. Dealing with someone's Conscious Mind can be dangerous. There must be a better way. So I had to ask how to deal with it.

It was only much later that I fully realized the truth that although all of us are indeed possessors of two very different minds, a Higher Mind of great beauty and grace and a Conscious Mind, which often harbors fear, we can chose which mind to use. I also found that there is a higher plan. We are fated to merge the two minds together in perfect cooperation. The Fearful One can be healed and learn to be peaceful as well, but it takes a much higher understanding through exploration of the Higher Mind. But, certainly, it is not necessary for one to give peace and to receive meanness over and over again. One who is in fear is guided by karma, which is an automatic feedback device steering them away from harm. Since they cannot be open to their Higher Mind, which would give them kindness, the painful consequences at least keep them from going over the cliff of total misery. Their fears manifest into fearful events and eventually turn them to look for something better. It's the same for all of us and we can only help the fearful ones to understand and make their own decision to avoid the Fearful One and accept the Peaceful One. Bottom line is that you do not have to suffer harm from a fearful one, you can entrust them to karma and pray for their Highest Good.

OK, I know that this only opens up more questions, so are you ready to delve into this reading, my friend? It is, indeed, a good place to start, but I warn you that it will lead you well past your current understanding of life. I know that it is uncomfortable to be such a pioneer of mind, but I just can't stop now. What if I could understand it and not live in misery? What if we all could? If I falter, please stop and help me and don't leave me now. I know that you can hear me now or you would have been too fearful to proceed.

Message from The Peaceful One

Living With the Higher Plane, 12.5.12

Peace and Light Association
Peaceandlight01@aol.com
PeaceandLight.net
Copyright 2012

Once entry has been made to the Higher Plane – sometimes by what seems a coincidence, random, or even by more profound experiences – there is a natural entry point or doorway that has been opened a bit wider by this first experience. Each succeeding experience further expands the opening and requires the necessary conditions of peace to be accomplished. However, this is only the beginning, as there are far more levels and even other entry points that can be developed. With that being understood, it is necessary to know how one has come to be in peace so that the entry system can advance.

Thus we are dedicating this reading to the need for a peace consciousness as obtained by some by the practice of meditation and by others as merely looking at peaceful scenes or listening to peaceful music. Once one has mastered the art of laying down the concerns of the Conscious Mind only to find that they were all attended to in the absence of attention, one is truly ready to invite the internal dialogue that has so much to offer. Even one who is much practiced might wonder exactly how one becomes a reader of one's own Higher Mind. However it is approached, it is likely to be the one and only activity that truly changes the lives of the practitioners.

First, there is the need to be trustworthy to enter into this dialogue. Therefore, setting the intention to be about the Highest Good and only the Highest Good needs to be set and reset from time to time. If one has this true intention, there are matters of the mind on the other end of the conversation that are to be attended to. Just as one must knock at the door of a friend before entering, so one must address the entity or resource with which one wants to interact. Thus, to say the name or color or feeling of energy is to address the entity. And in doing so, only that one will enter into the dialogue. Once one has favorite names to call each helper along the path, there is at once the favor of a reception of grace to be had.

As with any conversation, if one is at one level of understanding of what a conversation is about and the other has another understanding, there is the possibility that one might miss the other. Thus, there is the need to be addressing the friendliness issue – such as asking: "How are you?" In spirit form, there is a form of address known as "Speak intelligibly, and I will reply." In other words, be concise and direct. If you want to address the great resource for financial support, then ask for Financial Assistance – and respectfully and confidently think of them as responsive and helpful, and they will be so. If you expect them to never reply or to be so delayed that you die of the waiting, then do not bother – for there are none of those beings present on the other side. There are only those who need to be ever present, helpful and vigilant as to the satisfaction of your most dire or even your most simple needs.

In other words, the money to buy a million-dollar piece of land to demonstrate how crops can be grown without chemicals is as simple as asking for twenty-five cents for a parking meter. Trust and have confidence that you have addressed the most effective and efficient source for both advice and energy to be given to you for the formation of almost anything that you need. After some time of interaction with the many resources of help, you will develop a sort of contact list such as you would use for a cell phone or e-mail account. Each is very personal and private, and no two would probably read the same. Therefore, if you are very needful in many ways, take one at a time. And in accepting help with one concern, you will find that many other needs are also included in the transaction.

There is always the need to be in peace before signing off. Thus, we find that the prayer of the Beloved One Association has the right idea. Simply reciting The Lord's Prayer is sufficient, for it calls upon the ultimate Source and the Highest Good Intention to be present and bless both the petitioner and the resource giver. Thus, all are blessed and none are disrespected or harmed.

With this, we have written you many times with no way to address this issue so precisely, so we must be about the task of alerting you as to how we were able to access this particular experience at this moment.

For example, we find one who has often opened her heart to one to come and join her, but yet no response of value has been forthcoming. With this in mind, she has determined to just bless the person and situation with the prayer of the Heavenly Father to which most also ascribe. Thus, although there was no return response as of yet, the transaction was taken to its fullest and will be addressed as so. With this done, there is no need to explore any further.

Lest we say that one thing leads to another, there is yet another thing to explore on this topic. How would you have us address you? Are you the pathetic figure depicted as the Joyce of the early dialogues or are you the Enlightened One who writes the commentary? If you are the former, then your resistance to having good is too great, and we must wait until you open further. However, if you are the latter, then do not be concerned, for your needs will be addressed as soon as the conditions are peaceful. For those who have decided to have and intend only the Highest Good have also broached the access to the many wondrous levels of resources and types of communications available to them. For these, we find the need for yet another reading at a later time on the nature of these other levels and their access and proper use.

Thus, we find that none but the best effort has been given and so there remains only manifestations to be given, anything from the divine to the bovine, so to speak. As is the way with all manifestations, time and peaceful conditions are required and so, in finding a delay, do not give in to the urge to repeat and to re-explore the issue, just reiterate that the need has been given due attention and that nothing more is due until the time of its arrival, which might be as soon as now or as late as forevermore. In trusting that timeliness is of the essence in some situations, there is no more need to be revisiting that as well. Thus, we find that the Lifestyles of the Peaceful and the Patient are to be found on the Peace and Light Website for those who have trouble with this or any part of the transaction.

All of this being said, let it be known that the lower levels of experience opening to the Higher Realms are very user friendly, so to speak. Much effort is made to help each one reach their goal, even if it is so simple as to be made happier. In fact, there is a Happiness Retrieval Association to which many apply when in need and receive quite prompt and valid responses. For as soon as one says the words, "I want to be happy," all that is sad and harmful is immediately, or as soon as benignly possible, removed from their environment. It might be a partner, a spouse, a job, a friendship, or even an irritant to the skin.

When that is accomplished, then much grief relief will be experienced, which might take several weeks, months or even years to complete. These are not to be judged as good or bad, as the needs vary greatly. But once this is essentially complete and one decides that nothing disastrous happened except that one's life did get better by the removal of those at odds with their goals, one has accepted the first premise of the Higher Realm functioning in one's life.

Because we live in the Presence of God, all we experience and give is peace and love. We take no prisoners, nor do we resist any urge to help one to be good, happy, healthy, productive and all together a good citizen, parent, worker, or leader. Just ask for the Happiness Entry Point Captain who will lead you to all others associated with this activity that you might need.

With that taken care of, there is no need any better than the health of the body. The issues of bodily and emotional health are given much priority and those who have gained access, at once find that their urge for rest and rejuvenation is strongly felt. With that, we need to know that you are willing to cooperate with us, so just be compliant when you are given the prompting to relax, rest, and refresh yourself or to eat better or exercise more. If you do not comply, then another approach is given until one is found to which you will comply with comfort and promptness. Much can be gained by being in peace of mind, but even more by being in wellness and grace of form and figure.

Lastly, we have never been shy of being addressed with the worthy questions of the how and why of all things bright and beautiful such as this one delights to do and is so happy and blessed to be able to share with you, the delighted reader. We end this dialogue with just the thing for finding out for yourself how to enter and leave the

Higher Plane of existence, which is your home for all time. So don't be a stranger as we are your family of peace, sometimes called The Great Oneness, and we always leave the light on in the window for you to find your way home. Once you have entered we embrace you in peace, treat you with respect and love, and never give you any fright or demise of any kind.

Thus, we end this dialogue with the urging to all who have read this far: "Give us a call. Let's talk."

Commentary

Is this reading as amazing to you as it is to me? How can we hear each other so clearly and never have met? How could I sit down at a computer and relax my body and mind and be able to know in my mind such profound realities and then later have them show up in real life? Such is the nature of a connection to a pure mind, one not polluted by fear and grief. If you have tried a few more times to open to The Peaceful One, you may have found that it becomes easier and more clear the more you try. That is the way that it comes. It is like standing before a door trying to open it, fearing and doubting, only to find that if you just give it a confident push that it swings open.

Once inside, you have to leave your grief behind and change your mind about who you really are because you are in the company of very happy people. By grief, I mean that the remembered hurts of life experience and the doubting of oneself, which essentially can turn one's mind into a self-destruction machine, literally cutting oneself off from most of the life force and intelligence that one possesses in its higher, pure form. Look at it this way. Your fears are just a pair of muddy shoes. Kick them off and have a seat at the party.

I wonder how many others we could invite to the party. Would they be willing to kick off their shoes or would they grumble and stomp away leaving muddy tracks? Where does this pure mind of life force and intelligence exist so they could find it? How could one use it to change one's own life circumstances? Would it protect us from further bad experiences just by intending the Highest Good? If many did the same, how would the society change? Have there ever been societies on the Earth who tried to do this? What was their experience, and what happened to them? If they had access to pure mind, did they leave behind a trail for us to use to find their secrets? Or even better, did they leave instructions for how to proceed forward today – going beyond what even they achieved? Is that what the Egyptian wall paintings are all about? Do other traditions such as tribal legends, cultural myths, and living organizations such as the Masonic Traditions tell of similar events? Could we study them and find the footprints of the Highest Good in our history?

Can you, dear reader, find your pure mind and see your life change to the good and thereby push your part of society in the right direction? If others have done it, are you essentially any different? " If you said yes, you are right. And if you said no, you are right," as Henry Ford said. It is not a matter of ability or experience or meditating and fasting or confessing or even being good. Peacefully wanting to be happy and asking for guidance is the "only, only, did I say only?" criteria. I myself didn't get intent on finding it until I was miserable and had no other choice. Please do not wait that long, for it is not necessary. Even sitting by a sunny window watching birds feed is reason enough to say: "Oh, Peaceful One, speak to me, for I wish to be happier yet."

Step Three

Color: Apple Green
Stone: Green Topaz
Herb: Licorice
Scent: Mint
Musical Note: E
Physical/Emotional Response: Rest and Sleep

The dialogue

Almost a year has come and gone since we began this dialogue together, and the legal problems are coming to completion. With almost no effort or expense on my part, a peaceful solution to my every problem and settlement of all concerns as begun to take shape. I could truthfully say that I did almost nothing, but rest, sit in the sunny window, take naps and talk to the Peaceful One. It's as if I were in a different world exploring spiritual truths of life while everything else was on a pre-programmed track for the good. Was this the Highest Good at work in my life? Is this how the protection of the Highest Good works?

In getting used to the idea of the two minds, I just had to ask more questions to fully understand all that it means, so I had daily dialogues and of course, Dear Reader, you were there with me. I asked questions, but you should also ask them yourself. Your Peaceful One is ready to answer at any moment for we can all hear each other now. Don't falter now. Keep going. Surely by now you realize that only good can come of it.

+

Joyce: Dear Peaceful One, I am reporting for our dialogue again today. I have to laugh. I'm still sitting in the same sunny window a year later, and my life is slowly getting better. But I am so fascinated at what you are teaching me that I don't really care about the problems that seemed so disastrous a year ago. It's going to be all good, isn't it? Even if I do nothing?

Peaceful One: That is what you were told in the beginning and it is still true – and it will always be true for you and all others as well. The universe was programmed from the beginning by the Source, Who made it so. And that **Source is a good one Who created good** and nothing else.

Joyce: So there's nothing to fear?

Peaceful One: That's right. Nothing to fear unless you wish something to fear. Do not doubt it, for doubt turns your happiness into sorrow each time you turn to it.

Joyce: So why do we have fear at all if it's not real?

Peaceful One: If you are thinking that fear is not real unless one attends to it and that it can be eliminated rather easily by focusing on peace, you are correct. It is the result of a limited mind not seeing the whole picture, but having the full power of free will at its disposal, chooses what seems real in complete disregard to all that is apparent in the natural world.

How does a teenager feel when put behind the wheel of a very powerful car and has the freedom to drive it? Does he or she make many mistaken decisions and even create a wreck of it? Does he or she then have to get back behind the wheel and keep trying to understand how to control the car by reforming each decision based on the experience of the last crash?

Imagine yourself coming into physical existence in possession of a baby mind, not fully understanding itself. You would make many mistakes and your parents would protect you from the worst ones but let you take a few scrapes. You would learn quickly unless you were very stubborn indeed. In the end, even the stubborn ones have no other choice. They just take more scrapes to find their way. All are good minds seeking good lives. Your parents would not let you hurt your brothers or sisters nor destroy your own toys. They might send you to time-out. In such isolation and pain, you can revise your plan for your next adventure. In short you are growing up learning how to live here in peace. A wild ride to be sure.

From a higher understanding, however, fear exists as the need to procreate beings possessing free will. If one begins with good, then chooses fear, finally expanding into love, then love is brought to every part of the physical universe you call Earth. It is a show of light and love brought to you by your Great Oneness. In fact, there is a planning committee just for the Earth's experience. You will be hearing from them regarding what they have in store for the Earth's next experience.

Joyce: This should be good. I've heard about the fearful predictions regarding the year 2012. What's that all about? And what is this planning committee?

Peaceful One: By accessing your own Higher Mind, you have come to the point that you believe that all is good for you. What if that is in fact the intention of all who helped to found and guide life on Earth? These great spiritual beings had a plan for life on the Earth. All of the old spiritual traditions record some type of story of a great beginning on the Earth.

In fact, that plan is just coming to pass as people come to realize that their minds are their place of work. If they intend the Earth to be in peace, then it shall be. If they believe that it is in danger, then there will be the many setbacks caused by fear, greed and grief.

This is a point of great decision, which is what the year of 2012 is all about. You might think of it as marking the beginning of the end of fear. From now going forward, it is the plan for Peaceful Ones to heal all beings of fear. It is good that you have been brought to this point in your life when you can write this book and send it out to the world in digital form instantaneously so anyone who is looking for this type of information can easily find it. They can begin to incorporate it into their lives of happiness. It is no accident.

Joyce: Oh, I get it, that's what Edgar Cayce talked about as the soul's life plan before incarnation. It is part of our soul's plan to do this, right? And we are part of the big plan for the Earth to be at peace by eliminating fear. And we volunteered to go through the fears in order to finish growing up ourselves and to have compassion for others trying to build a better life. We are a small part of a big plan for the Earth to be at peace by overcoming fear. My part was to write about it and Dear Reader planned to read it so others could understand as well. Right? So sweet! Surely we are not the only ones?

Peaceful One: As you guessed, there are many others who have come with the same purpose for we are all One and have the same destiny that is good. Would you like to hear from some of them?

Joyce: You're kidding! You mean that I can talk to other souls and hear them just like I hear you? Would that include hearing my Dear Reader?

Peaceful One: How peaceful would that be! It would seem that the Higher Plane is a very interesting place to explore. Yes, there are many like yourselves in existence, some in soul form only and some in both soul and physical form. Since we were all created from the original Source, which was good, then we are all good and seek only good. There is no separation, so all of them have been listening to you and are willing to talk to you about how you can manifest good. We all love to make things good. So ask away and see what you get.

Joyce: I'm going to ask for someone I know, so I can attest to the reader that it is not a fake. How about my mother who is dead? Can I talk to her?

Mothering One: My dearest little one: How dear you are to me. I remember how I would call you to come and help me with the other children, and you would come so willingly. I remember how we sat and read stories together. Do you remember the story of The Contented Little Pussy Cat? It was your favorite because your father bought it for you. You learned to read so fast. When you went to school, I applied makeup to the birthmark on you face so you would not be embarrassed at school. I have so much to tell you about your childhood.

Joyce: Oh, my God. I can't believe it. I know that it is you, Mother. Only you would know this, and it makes me feel like you are back here with me now. I've missed you so. No one loved me like you did. I don't know what to say. What do you want to say to me?

Mothering One: I know that you have felt unloved since I left physical existence and that it affected your life profoundly, especially your relationships. So I want you to know that you are learning the final lessons of growing up that I started to teach you. You are beautiful beyond belief, and you do not need to suffer or accept second best. If you have confidence in yourself and always choose what is good for you, and all will work out well for you.

Joyce: I now can see how you saw me as a daughter, and I am so grateful for your love. It is deep and strong enough to carry me forward. I never thought about having to continue growing up. How do I do that?

Mothering One: You have found your source of guidance for the good. Listen to that guidance, for it will take you every step of the way. You will do many good things, and I am always very proud of you.

Joyce: I feel so grateful for you.

Peaceful One: Then more good things for which to be grateful will come to you. That is the birthright that every mother gives to her children. I gave you the great gift of first being loved in this physical world. I saw who you really are and loved you. It is but a small taste of the great Source Who made you. Think about this for a while.

Joyce: I'm usually not speechless, but for now I am. All that I can suggest is that you take a minute, Dear Reader, and write a letter to yourself about the experience of first love. Perhaps it was your mother, father or maybe someone else. See where it takes you. Here is mine.

+

A letter to myself:
The Gift of First Love

What could be better than to find that the flowers and birds of a sunny field on a peaceful afternoon are the gift of love? Who could have sent them to me, or rather me to them? I think none but my first love, for I would not have recognized love as such without the first opening of my heart.

What beloved baby cannot help but know that its heart beats strong and that its breath is sure because of the gift of life from its parents? How carefully it is fed and enfolded in strong arms. None but the strong love of a mother for her infant can set a child on a long path of strength. How many people take even forgotten and abandoned babies and give them love in their homes? How many teachers foster the growth of a good mind temporarily low on self-confidence? How many coaches and leaders give the gift of self-esteem?

How can I thank one so strong to have carried and nurtured me? That love was shown through many sorrowful events of her life and despite the doubts and failings of later years. How can I do the same for others? How could so much good come from giving a kind remark or taking care of a sick, discouraged or injured one? They are everywhere, and they all need a sip of that love to awaken and sustain them. This is how we launch the path to peace. It is impelled by the acts of love that we do for each other. In giving love, I learn that I am, too, a first love giver for many. And it is a good thing, even if the gift of a drop of love is not understood or even rejected. For in being a giver of love, I have engaged my soul in once again creating a thing of beauty: a life that can stand in love.

I thank you all who have loved me. And I give once again my love to all who have offended me. I may have to stay at a distance from you, for you still want to harm me, but within my heart, you are loved – for I am a loving being of strength. Those who are waiting for me to show up on my path with love in my heart: I will not fail you. I will proceed with forgiveness and a willing heart, and I will know you when I meet you.

+

These moments spent in conversation with my mother, or for you it might be another, cannot be underestimated. They have a way of healing. All choices in the future will have to be different. We can't give our attention to the Fearful One anymore. We have better things to do. But we will need some expert guidance. We don't want to get off of the peaceful track, so resolve to listen to the Peaceful One each moment of the day.

Dear Reader, have you ever felt a shiver on your back when you thought of a departed loved one? Those faint feelings of energy moving on our skin are there when a presence is giving you a hug. Open your mind to the possibility that you can hug back by just saying, "Hello. I've missed you. Let's talk." You will know who it is, for you heart does not forget a touch or a smell or the sound of a loving thought. Wouldn't a loved one just love to be loved back? I'm not sure, but I think my porcelain angel just smiled at the thought that we might all be living among loved ones who can come when we think of them and continue to love us forever. I wonder what else she thinks is coming for us. Since love is the heartbeat of God, we can safely assume that it will not stop or fail to exist in any time or place. Finding that love is, in fact, our Highest Good, fortunately, it's not far away. Look how close we have become since you started to read this book. I can hear you and you can hear me. We are all safe in the Highest Good so we can afford to love each other. So can everyone else.

+

Just two days after the final court hearing and closure of the divorce, I got a call to return to work that offered me an easy schedule, good people to work with and excellent pay. I now had a car in good working order to use that was in my name. Everything that I needed was there. Surely it is a fulfillment of the prediction that all would work out well if I just trusted that all would be good.

+

Joyce: Dear Peaceful One, now that my mind is made up to be my true self, a Beloved One and a Giver of Love, and not to be fearful, how are we going to do this?

Peaceful One: Well, there is just one more thing that I might explain to you before we move on. There is not just one right thing or wrong thing. Don't judge any decision for any reason except that it is peaceful for you and all others. Let's explore the meaning of the Highest Good.

Joyce: Dear Peaceful One, before we do that, one last question. Are you my soul or someone else? Are you God? How is it that I know you?

Peaceful One: I am indeed your soul. Are you amazed at how wise and beautiful we are? I'm here because I am you and you are me. In fact, let's just call it us, for we are now able to be of one mind. I am not God, but I live within God just as you live within me. In fact, I gave birth to your mind just like your parents did for your physical body. I will not and can't leave you.

Joyce: Oh, I get it. You are like my mother and father and you love me.

Peaceful One: Such is the case and it is the same for all humans, no exceptions.

Joyce: So are you telling me that my Dear Reader is also hearing from his or her own soul? You are saying that all souls are joined together in peace so they are all Peaceful Ones.

Peaceful One: That is so. The Peaceful Ones are called the Great Oneness and they are always creating good. Isn't it good that you opened the door and entered into the dialogue with your own true self of pure and good mind?

Joyce: OK, you and me and Dear Reader, we set out to be happy, so let's proceed onward. I know that good has come to me with little effort – and much better than if I had tried it myself, so I have to go forward in the same way and ask: "How did we create all of this good? " This part of me sure doesn't know.

Peaceful One: First, let's get a few pronouns right. There are within each human two minds. One is a Higher Mind, which is the soul. And the other is the Conscious Mind, a small projection of the Higher Mind that has a very limited perspective due to the fact that it is living in time and space where things

63

happen one event at a time, not all at once like on the soul side. We showed you the quote from Einstein: "The only reason that we have time is so that everything doesn't happen all at once." So we refer to ourselves as plural, but actually we are all one and even if we have very different perspectives, we are essentially one.

Joyce: So I think of me, meaning my Conscious Mind, as a small part of my soul that can only know things one thing at a time, whereas, the soul can know everything all of the time?

Peaceful One: Yes, and unless you can access your Higher Mind and see from that higher perspective, you can see only a very small part of existence. This condition fosters doubt because you cannot see the good ahead of you nor the vast amount of help that is available to you. I can help you from the bigger and higher perspective, like standing on a hill rather than in a valley. We call the small perspective mind the Conscious Mind because you are conscious of it most of the time, but it is the least capable of the two.

Joyce: Ok, I don't get all of this, but I'll go along with it because I know that it is so much better than living in the dark valley. What's next?

Peaceful One: Take a walk with me, and I will show you what the trail has to offer and how to find level ground, good water and places to live. For I can see what is available for you, and I made a good plan for you. I planned for you to be happy. I have only the Highest Good in mind for you. If you also adopt the intention for the Highest Good, then we work together perfectly and only good can result. Once again, we remember the story that the Bible tells about the Good Shepherd.

I cannot make your choices for you, for that is your experience to have, much like the teenager learning to drive a car, but I can guide you from a good place. Think of me, and all others like us, as "Friends in High Places." Sit quietly and peacefully each day and listen and I will send you messages of good guidance. Then we would walk the path together and bring that love that you were talking about to others on the way.

Joyce: You make it sound so simple and good. Has it always been like this for humans?

Peaceful One: At one time, we were on Earth only in spirit form and then later we chose to live in animal bodies, which required the formation of the Conscious Mind. You'll find it all described in the Edgar Cayce books. At all times, there was the abiding presence of the Christ Consciousness and His great love for all beings on the planet. He decreed that all should be loved, no exceptions. And He even came to demonstrate that principle through a life lived in Palestine.

He intended for life on Earth to be good, so He taught you to open to your Higher Minds by praying the Our Father. In its many different cultural versions, it says the same thing. We all came from the same Source, which is good, and that good is given each day in small steps, so you can and should forgive and love one another. In short, if you ask for good to be given and the guidance to give love each day, it will be lavished on you just as you have been given life itself.

As you grow in love, you become more and more in cooperation with God. We think of the Highest Good as moving into the Presence of God, where you originated, much like being loved by your mother who gave you physical birth. Each day, we give you guidance for your Highest Good. We want nothing but that for any being.

Joyce: We're getting pretty deep here, but I think I know what you mean. So what is my Highest Good for today?

Peaceful One: Let's take the peace and quiet of this sunny window experience with you to your place of work tomorrow and do your best each day to help the company you work for do good for all of its employees, customers and, vendors. That would help with the Highest Good for many people.

Joyce: You mean that even working at a company is a part of all of this?

Peaceful One: Yes, nothing is excluded. We'd like you to see that any organization which seeks to achieve good, is a giver of good for all who are associated with it. They use the rich reserves of energy in the universe of good, and they give out all manner of good to many who interact with them. It is only required that they remove fear and harm no one so as to invest only in good. The more that they do this, the more peaceful and productive they are, the more good is created.

All creation is a manifestation of the Great Source of Existence, and you are a great being of grace wherever you go. So yes – be yourself every moment of your life, and we will be there to help you to understand and to find good things to chose for yourself as well as for all others. Then all can live in peace, and the Earth can be healed so that our mission here will be finished. Then, we might just all take a vacation and go somewhere else for a long rest.

Joyce: So you mean to say that the Earth has been ruled by fear for a long time, and now it is the time to lose the fear and live in peace? That sounds like a huge project. There are so many people who are fearful.

Peaceful One: That is so, but it would take only the choice to open up to one's Higher Mind to make all of the difference. Higher Mind is the access point to the giving of great good. And that includes much that is highly technical. For example, in ancient Egypt they used their Higher Minds in a very methodical way and were given technical solutions for living in peace together – and so they prospered very well. Relying on the Conscious Mind would never have achieved what they were able to do by being peaceful and doing nothing for periods long enough to hear their own Higher Minds. They applied the Highest Good to building a society, building pyramids, healing illness, and doing business.

Joyce: So is ancient Egypt an example of a culture based on the guidance of the Higher Mind? I remember that Cayce talked a lot about that culture. How they built the Great Pyramid is still a mystery today, even with our highly technical skills and tools. So you say they got their technology from accessing their Higher Mind? I read once that many great inventors got their best ideas while sleeping.

Peaceful One: Yes, in sleep the body belongs totally to the Higher Mind, and so it is refreshed and renewed each night. In addition, the Conscious Mind is at rest, so only the Higher Mind is active and often leaves some great information in the form of dreams, which the Conscious Mind can remember and try to understand.

Joyce: So that is why I've been sleeping so much. You are healing my body and sending messages in the form of dreams. When I am awake, you are educating and guiding my Conscious Mind. Wow!

+

How can I express how loved I began to feel even though I was living alone and divorced, and until very recently, unemployed. How could so much good come from so little effort? Have you ever been truly loved? Have you come to mistrust love? Did you close your heart so you will not be hurt again? If it were safe to love, would you open up again? Imagine what it would be like if you could face a fearful experience and then look back to see that everything turned out OK. It might be that way if you trusted the Highest Good to bring you good.

I had learned to trust this guidance, but how did I know that it was true unless I realized that I was given so much good in actual manifestations? Everyone knows when he or she is being loved. And deep down we know that we are supposed to be loved as it is our true nature. Fearful experiences are the only way that we can become confused and possibly believe that we need to be treated badly, are in danger or are worthless.

This world of fear is a tricky thing indeed. I can't believe my good luck as to have found my way out of it intact. I could have recycled through fearful experiences for my whole life – or even many lifetimes, if Cayce is to be believed. Since he lived in modern times, I came to think of him as the great door opener of the Higher Mind, and I referred to his readings often to learn what he communicated while in sleep trance. Indeed, I found that he had lived in ancient Egypt in a prior life and in that lifetime, founded that great civilization based on access to Higher Mind. I could only guess that he came to this time and place once again to see if we wanted to do it again. In fact, there are many of us who were present with him in ancient times and have come back with him in the present. We would have a sense of delight in helping with this effort, I'm sure. Of course, we would all need to be healed ourselves of our fears and illnesses to be of any help, but then most of his readings were about healing. So I assume that he left these for us to use to heal ourselves and get on with our work.

The part about sleep really interested me. I had read that the human body had two nervous systems: one under conscious control of the will, and the other not. It seemed logical that each functioned in coordination with each of the two minds. If we relax the Conscious Mind or when we go to sleep, the Higher Mind will take over the perfection of the body through its own nervous system. Only the

Conscious Mind uses its nervous system to fill the body with the toxins of fear, which induce the body to disease and aging. Left under the influence of Higher Mind, I guess that we would live in health much longer.

But once we experience illness and aging, can it be reversed? I wanted to remember to ask for a reading on this important matter at a later time. For I was born in 1945, the same year that Cayce died. I have been very healthy, but I was showing signs of aging for sure. What about others who suffer cancer and heart disease and many other problems? Our society is full of illness and aging. Was it all a result of fear? If we are all great Beings of Light, how does this all work out? I could see some of it in my small life experiences, but what about others and even our whole society? How could so many be helped from so small a beginning?

Dear Reader, apparently you and I are Beings of Light as well as flesh and blood. Especially if we scrape away the effects of fear, we glow just like the sun with colors of light so fine that they are beyond the visible range. Apparently we can be healed and rejuvenated by removing the effects of fear and asking for the Highest Good to be done in our body. After all, when we are afraid, we ask the opposite of health and get it. We ask to be made weak and lacking in life and light when we are fearful and sure enough we get sick and old. The better choice is to refuse to be fearful and to ask for more life and light. If we are peaceful, we are in contact with the Higher Mind where light and life is freely given. I know, it sounds simplistic, but I bet if I ask the Peaceful One to explain it more deeply, that it would be explained so that I can understand. Even though I don't know a lot about the science of light, I want to know more. I would love if you would go there with me. We could ask the Peaceful One to explain how we are made of light. Wouldn't that be fun and useful? Need a light to guide the way? Sit in a sunny window for a while and you'll find that they left the light on for you, too

Message from The Peaceful One

Life as Light, 12.1.12

Peace and Light Association
Peaceandlight01@aol.com
PeaceandLight.net

This reading is from one of the Great Ones who works with you at night in deep sleep. It was given in advance of the need to be used, and all of the preparation was made years before so that it could be transmitted in such a way that it could be both understood and would indeed give blessings for all who came to read it. So let us proceed without interruption from the Conscious Mind.

First there was light. And light was made into a word. And that word was peace. And that peace was made into a man who came to be known as Jesus Christ. With that word, He made a world of grace possible. He gave his followers his peace, and they recorded it for all future generations to read. He said that peace is the way to the truth and the light.

The truth is that light was the beginning of all life in the physical plane. At once known as the sun disk, the image of light was always a wonder in the sky, but unknown to man until today is the great secret of how light created a physical universe in which human bodies came to exist.

Light is thought of as being particles in motion, but it is much more. Light is the impulse of the Great Source of Creation to send forth its love into physical form. The impulses resonate at certain frequencies to create this or that in the physical world. And so it is that light frequencies will be the study of the future of mankind.

To understand a human being and its body, it is necessary to see it as the work of an impulse of light first sent from the Divine Heart, so to speak. More than a great thought, it was the first progeny of a great lover who loved to love. Coming from this pure Source of love, one's body is fashioned out of pure vibration set in motion by the will of a man and woman to have a child, which is able to proceed onward through life as an independent being capable of being made into a giver of life itself. Soon more information will be given about light amplification and how it can be used for the production of the Highest Good.

For example, as brain waves are the reflection of a mind at work in flesh and blood, it will become obvious that a thought is indeed a thing in the making. It starts as a wave of energy in a brain and ends in action. Should one be about the business of light amplification, one can be making much more of the world of physical existence that is creative, giving more life in pure reflection of the original giving of light. Light amplification is merely the art of taking the gift of life and turning it over and over until a new and more beautiful being emerges, much like procreation and development of a new child.

If one needed to be an amplifier of light, one might become human just for the experience as a being of grace in love with its Source and wanting to be an ever better reflection of that original grace. And so the human body is such a grace in constant motion. Around each human body is a subtle field of light, which cannot usually be seen by the eye, but which can be detected by instruments or seen by the visual intelligence resident in the human mind called the third eye. Thought to reside between and above the two eyes, the seat of visual intelligence is marked by a dot or a jewel in some cultures, but actually it inhabits the mind and images are given to the brain by us to be expressed in mental images. The Higher Mind can give an image to this

73

visual intelligence as a way to communicate. This is what dreams are.

These subtle fields of energy, much like weak magnetic fields, surround all beings and are often called the aura field. Even the Earth has an aura to be seen in the northern sky under certain conditions. These fields of light move in accord with thought patterns and never leave a trace behind unless a thought is held firmly for a long time. Thus, a brief thought of peace leaves a weak field, but if held long enough, feeds the body with the love energy of peace. In the case of a human aura, the body eventually conforms to that shape and vibration, creating a body of peace. Let's refer to this aura field and the body contained within it as the Body of Light.

Once this Body of Light has a field of peace established, it flourishes for much longer than one might think possible. It continually feeds and is nourished by the original intention for a beautiful life given by the Creator. Thus, without the distortion of fear, a body is always in love with itself as a reflection of the original Creator. And thus it lives forever unless relinquished at will for the purpose of re-creating an even better experience.

When a body is asleep, it refreshes itself at the fount of all life, and it is encouraged to reform itself into its original design. During sleep, all information from the Higher Plane is available in undiluted form. And thus when Cayce fell asleep and responded to questions, he was able to do as Plato did and drink from the fountain of truth and guidance and bring it back for all to hear. What people heard were words that informed them of their true state of being, to be healthy and to reflect the light of a divine existence that nourishes and sustains them in all ways. When one goes to sleep with a certain attitude or intention to recall the experience, one can recall a dream. A dream is a sequence of visual images evoking great emotion, which

74

stimulates a strong desire to understand the intelligence that has given it to them.

When requested, the body can rejuvenate and heal itself from this great fount of life expressed in light. Therefore, the nature of the light body is the major interest of healers of all types and kinds. Therefore, the nature of vibration and resonance needs to be studied, for all beings of light vibrate and resound themselves in many different ways. They all leave traces of their song wherever they go. Thus, by recording these songs or resonances in blocks of rock, crystallized stone, or even sand, the entire history of that place and time is left to be decoded and soon will be.

Thus the body resonates in tune with the pure mind of its original Creator, unless influenced by long-standing fear. The process of healing and rejuvenation is essentially the removal of fear. There are many resonances such as color, stones, plants, scents, and music, which literally shake off the fears and retune the body of light. Thus much has been explained about the term light and much more will be given when the time is right and the students appear.

Let it be noted here that there is nothing to fear but fear itself, as Franklin D. Roosevelt once said, for fear binds the heart and closes the passages of peace and life energy. Without fear, life would adjust to all occurrences with peace and joy – and therefore health and well being would continue. And so it comes to the forefront as to how to have a life without fear, and that is the topic of the following stages. For now, let's see what commentaries have transpired, followed by a new dialogue.

Commentary

Do you feel like shouting Whoopee? OK, I know that you have to think about what has been said, but first rejoice because we are free. We are free to be healthy, happy and, prosperous. And it can and does happen. Once a mind has been made up to be at peace, there is an unfoldment that happens. First, there is a settling of old debts by reviewing one's life. That may take a long time and even be reviewed over and over later, but the final outcome is that all of one's life must be seen in a peaceful way. This first unfoldment means that nothing of guilt or blame needs to be suffered, and that there is only good to be had if one only asks for it. In this process, the issues of the karmic life are resolved in peace.

Following this unfoldment, there is an initial opening of the heart in the recalling of good, loving experiences, in particular the first loving as parents do for their children. Once the heart admits that maybe things have been a confusing mixture of both good and bad and that the bad can be dealt with peacefully, then the whole world of enlightenment begins to be made available. And with that event being called a blessing, the purposeful requesting of good begins to take hold of the life experience. This fulfills the belief that if one is positive and insists that good will come from every experience, then life proceeds down a path to much good.

Did you know that you glow in colors? From the cosmic view, the edited version of this progress is held in a color code. Thus, those on the etheric side of life can look at the emanations of one's aura and tell what stage of existence one has achieved and what intentions are at work. Thus, some are attracted to be of help when certain colors and patterns appear, and others wait until a more opportune time when the color is right. Thus there are, at moments of great peace, the dreams, the whisperings of good to be had within one's mind. If one recognizes it as one's soul talking to one's own cousin, the Conscious Mind, then the dialogue arises. If it is believed to be real, there is a greedy desire to know more. But if there is doubt, then it will cease. Even Cayce, who produced his readings during sleep, had great doubt and dread about his readings and what they were saying. He proceeded with them only because he saw that the remedies given to sick people were doing so much good, and that is what he wanted to do with his life and his talent. And thus it was so.

Indeed, the body portrayed as a light bulb is a good one. The light is energized by the flow of electricity, and the light exceeds the bounds of the glass bulb – flowing outward in all directions. It is a really good explanation of the seed of life that was given to us. If one would paint the bulb a fearful black with only a few scratches of clearness, it would not give much light and get very hot inside, eventually burning out. And so it is with our health. By rubbing out the fear and grief, the light can flow outward as it was designed to do. And as long as our life energy flows, we will continue to radiate according to the original gift of life, which was a great one.

Are you thinking the same thing I am? I would love to invite researchers and healthcare professionals who wish to participate to form study groups to research the Higher Mind for more information about how health and peaceful ways of living on this planet can be maintained and illness and social problems reversed so we can test and implement the advice and see what good can be obtained. It will be a lot of work and time, but all would be living under the intention for the Highest Good and will be giving and receiving grace and light, so we will receive all of the good that we are seeking and then give it away. That would be very blissful indeed.

Dear Reader, I know that you may not care too much for dusty Egyptian tombs or old libraries, but I've heard you many times ask about your own health and safety and that of your loved ones. Thus I will press on, asking about how things of good and not-so-good happen in our lives. If you want to ask about a special concern, just ask your own Peaceful One and let me know for I want to hear as well.

Step Four

Color: Blue Green
Stone: Opal
Herb: Sage
Scent: Dandelion
Musical Tone: F
Emotional/ Physical Reaction: Activity, Harmonious Excitement

The dialogue

Joyce: So, let me ask a really scary question. Just how much influence does the Higher Mind have on us and our everyday experiences?

Peaceful One: Most everything and every moment except what the Conscious Mind selects or changes into a setback. Higher Mind gives loads of good every minute, but you can choose with your free will to accept it or change it. What a good reason to open to your Higher Mind. It's a happening place, so to speak.

Joyce: So let me get this straight. There are entities of all kinds and interests in the Great Oneness who can communicate to us and are always giving good?

Peaceful One: Right.

Joyce: And some of them have lived a physical life like I am doing, and some not?

Peaceful One: Right.

Joyce: Do they know everything?

Peaceful One: Yes. They all know everything that you and each person who has ever lived has experienced and known, and they remember it and can tell it all back to you. Cayce referred to this library of information as the Akashic Record. In ancient times, books on readings from this Great Oneness were stored in the Library of Alexandria and were available to anyone who wanted to come and study them.

Some of the Great Oneness have particular interests, so just ask for what you need and those interested in that topic will respond. They will identify themselves gladly and even refer you on to others if more help is needed. To use an analogy, it is a huge spiritual internet with everyone online all of the time.

Joyce: Wow. I had no idea. I suppose you are suggesting that my request acts like a search engine to find what I need in the spirit world. Hah! I think I'll call it Spoogle. How many other people know about this?

Peaceful One: At certain times in Earth's history, it was well known, and others not so well. At present, it is looked at with suspicion, so not too many people inquire, but they will soon.

Joyce: Why is that? Is something bad going to happen?

Peaceful One: Quite the opposite. The few who dare to tread into this vast Oneness will be doing some remarkable things, and others will want to know more. Good has a habit of attracting attention. Look at what good has happened to you. Has it gotten you to pay attention?

Joyce: OK, I see your point.

Peaceful One: And why do you think that it is scary to be part of the Oneness?

Joyce: I thought that I had control over my life experiences.

Peaceful One: You do. You can choose what kind of thoughts to entertain, keeping in mind that they will proliferate and then you will have to deal with the outcomes of that choice. Fear begets more fear and peace begets more peace. Your great mind is highly creative.

Dealing with us is like playing cards. We shuffle the deck and deal. You pick up your hand of cards and play a card of fear and we play a card of peace to bring you back to peace. If you play a card of peace, we play another card of peace until you have a full house. We are highly reliable in that regard, but you and your partners can play as many fear cards as you like until you change your mind.

Joyce: I don't want to play any more fear cards. It hurts too much.

Peaceful One: Good decision. I wish that the populations of the Earth would do the same. Everyone would be a winner.

+

Two years after I started this dialogue, I was earning very good money. I bought a beautiful new car from my earnings. It was flashy red, just like I had always wanted, with a big sunroof so I could enjoy a sunny window as I drove. I had a new circle of friends, who were kind and helpful and, yes, they knew about the Good Friends in High Places, for they had learned how to access their Higher Minds as well. They were doing amazing things. I was happier and healthier than I had been in many years.

I also had a tall stack of handwritten notebooks containing all of the long conversations that I had with the Peaceful One.

At some point, I asked the Peaceful One to give me the gift of teaching others how to open to their Higher Minds as well, and I was given The Long Story. It is a simple but profound teaching tool. I hope you have already read it. If not, you will find it after Step Five with the Lord's Prayer.

I asked so many questions, that I now have a cache of readings on all kinds of topics that I can share with you if you have a mind to do so. Some of them are in this book, but others can be found on the website from time to time. I plan additional books in the Highest Good series, so watch for them. Later, we will sponsor conferences on different topics so like-minded people can meet and share their interests.

But beyond all of that, Dear Reader, I give you the greatest gift of all: I give you the gift of knowing how to find your own Peaceful One. Find a sunny window or any peaceful place, and relax your mind and your heart. Get very peaceful, and ask for your Highest Good for today – knowing that you are loved and waiting to hear from the one who loves you. Then wait until you get an answer that is loving and peaceful. Of the many who have tried, some have received images or songs or even feelings. I encourage all who want to Spoogle to accept what their search engine provides, look it over and then Spoogle further until it becomes even more clear and you can access it easily and consistently. Keep your mind very open to what you will get.

Remember that if you do not continue to try the peaceful way, then you will recycle through karmic experiences until you eventually find it. I had to recognize that I could have as many poor marriages as I wanted, or I could take the time to listen for some good guidance and succeed much better. There is no way to fail, but there clearly is an easy way and a hard way. Would you accept my gift of this book and give the easy way a good long effort?

If you get the Fearful One, stop and try again when you are more peaceful. Keep trying, and don't give up. Even though it will take some time to get good at it, there is so much good to be gained and so much pain to be avoided that it will be well worth it. It might only take you an hour, but it took me at least a year. However as I look back, I think that I was doing it all of my life in some form, but not recognizing what it was. Actually, it could have been done in a second, but I had to quiet the Fearful One, open my mind and learn how to recognize the Peaceful One. That's what took so long.

+

Joyce: How come in my dialogues I sound like my old self and the commentaries are by a more enlightened form of me? I thought that enlightenment was some rare state of bliss that one could reach only after practicing meditation or yoga for many years.

83

Peaceful One: At what point is a light bulb called enlightened? Once you were placed into existence so long ago as to make time a joke, you were enlightened and will always be so. What the great teachers were doing was to guide their students to release their fears and to realize that fear was the only thing keeping them from realizing that they were enlightened all along.

Maybe you can enlighten me on a certain topic. Why are you calling yourself the old Joyce when you are in fact realizing that you are enlightened?

Joyce: I guess I don't know. Would it be OK to refer to myself as an Enlightened One? I feel embarrassed to do so. I know myself to be so fallible. I wouldn't make a good example for others.

Fearful One: What's in a name, you can only be what you can be, whatever that is.

Joyce: Fearful One! I haven't heard from you for a long time, but I recognized you immediately. You sound different.

Peaceful One: Were you surprised to hear from the Fearful One once again? Did you notice how much less negative the Fearful One is these days? She is learning to trust and finds less reason for fear and separation. These are signs of healing. So let's peel off some more fear and see what we can do for her.

Joyce: Well, OK, but I don't get what's going one here.

Peaceful One: What you are getting is a grand opportunity to reunite all parts of yourself into one beautiful light bulb of peace. How does that sound?

Joyce: Cool! What would that feel like?

Peaceful One: It feels like a great amount of baggage is lifted from you, and you can leave it all on the conveyor belt of life and walk away free. It's like flying the friendly skies without even the airplane.

Joyce: Good, you are giving me an analogy. You're saying that I get to let go of the fear and grief baggage that I have been carrying most of my life and get on with my journey light and free.

+

Dear Reader, do you chuckle as I do, remembering standing in the airline baggage claim department time after time, watching everybody's bags go by while we wait for our own to come around? I suppose that we look eagerly for our grief baggage because they are familiar, and we think that we need them to carry on our journey. Indeed they have become the definition of who we are. Sigh, I wonder how many lifetimes we've had some of these old bags of grief. They are all pretty beat up, ugly, patched, smelly and sad looking. I'd sure like to unload that old brown bag of self-doubt and the backpack of childhood misunderstandings. And look at all of the other people's bags. These bags amount to a lot of human suffering and they go round and round until someone claims them. Can you recognize your own grief grips? Would you like to leave them behind and walk away? Good

85

thing these days we have decided to buy a ticket to better experiences. It feels good to travel light, doesn't it?

I wonder what it would be like to have no baggage at all. I promise to drop some of my baggage if you do too. Are you up for this? Grab my hand and we will do it together. There, drop the red one of anger and the brown one of guilt and regret and also the anxiety backpack from childhood. I'm letting go of the twin bags of relationship failures. Do you have anything else you would like to discard? I know that at first we are wondering if we will even recognize ourselves without the baggage, but that feeling will pass. Let's board the plane to happy vacations. That sounds like more fun and we won't look back.

+

Peaceful One: Having an analogy discussion with you is a good teaching tool, and we love the humor as well. It makes your light shine all the brighter.

Which part of you has been dark, just one or all? We'd like to propose that once you have dismissed the dark and dreadful thinking, that you see that all of you is a good and viable expression of the gift of life – living and breathing and doing all sorts of good and beautiful things. So just embrace yourself, and enjoy your life. For once you set the intention of the Highest Good for the rest of your life, you have unified your thinking with all of the rest of creation. And it will carry you with its mighty flow of energy. Come fly with us, so to speak.

Joyce: Well, then what kind of work or activity should I do?

Peaceful One: It's not so much that one is better than another, but that you love and enjoy one more than another. If you let your love for an activity lead you, you will experience joy. And the joy has a great deal of energy. The color of joy is yellow, so your aura will glow yellow and then later gold. Once you have begun to glow gold, then something else takes place.

Joyce: What's that?

Peaceful One: It will become evident.

+

OK, now the Peaceful One had my curiosity even more, but didn't immediately satisfy it. Maybe, something else was taking place. I wondered what it was. I tried to find out by asking more questions, but nothing worked. The Peaceful One was not saying anything until I asked my really great question: "What is the higher understanding?" Then I got the following reading. The Peaceful One was expecting me to think for myself in a positive way and to enjoy the ride into the wild blue. From here on out, it was required that I ask a valued or important question to get my answers. It was like being a loved companion, partnering up with a Great Wise One who had someplace to go and was taking me along and loving it. I liked it. I loved it. Don't be shy, it's easy and fun.

The reading that follows is amazing in that it is suggesting that instead of trying to work through every thought and fear in order to clear away the paint on the light bulb, so to speak, that one can just set the intention that one's thoughts are always golden. What golden thoughts are, I'm not quite sure, but it is good. Read along with me, and we can ask more questions later.

Message from The Peaceful One

Releasing Fear, 1.4.13

Peace and Light Association
Peaceandlight01@aol.com
PeaceandLight.net
Copyright 2013

Once one has determined to be sure of one's exit to the other side of misery, there is the matter of the fears that block the way. Many of these have been in place so long that they have literally determined the definition of one's self. Literally is quite the right term because it results in a firmly held name for oneself such as One Running Out of Time in Life to be A Success, or One Who Cannot Find the Right Spouse, or One Who Cannot Understand These Directions, etc. Once these names have been accepted and held to be part of oneself, there are comparable limitations and restrictions that one comes to accept about oneself. Without any limitation, one would be quite different, or at least one might assume so if one even had an idea of what that would be like.

Less than being in love with being one's true self would not suffice for breaking through these self-definitions. And so when one comes to a moment in life when frustration rises and causes an overflow of angry emotion, one has a small idea of the need for forgiveness to occur. According to our definition, forgiveness does not need to be given at all. It is simply the redefinition of the self as one who has not been harmed and never shall be. For without the ability to be harmed, there is an unlimited amount of good that can be had with little or no effort. Thus, we find that there is yet another way to proceed.

Instead of trying to determine each fear, its source and effect, it is so much better to merely ask that it be removed so that more good can come in and flood oneself with grace so strong as to refuse fear ever again. With that, one has a whole new meaning for the word strong. Would one be strong if one resisted an influence in any direction? Would one be strong if one persisted in the face of adversity and finally succeeded? Would one be strong if one carried on alone without help and succeeded? Would one be strong if one could devour all good things in such a quantity that one died from the effort? Would one be strong if one endured deprivation to the extent that nothing mattered at all? Would one be joylessly detached and be any happier? Nothing could be farther from the truth. Where the strength comes from is rather the problem to consider.

If one has a lifetime of reversals and then succeeds at something important enough to make one worthy of regard, would one then be strong? Or would it be better to think that even in the adversities and reversals that there was something at work that had more strength than a personality, something that flowed and gained in strength just because one participated in it? Would it seem fruitful to be part of a bigger whole and to find that no one ever was alone and without help? Such a Source would be quite a comfort. For if one trusted a person to help them and they then betrayed them, but the help still came in even stronger than before, then the betrayer had no real power. Even if one's grief and anger were strong for a while, there is still the confidence that there is another of greater strength to turn to. In fact, if someone disturbs your peace, just silently think: "It is time for you to go. Go and find your peace and do not disturb mine." Such words said silently in your peaceful heart causes the universe to move to make it so. What wise words it was to say: "Consider the source." The Higher Mind is that source of such great strength that it causes the sun to shine.

Even if your first love was there and presenting the gift of great love and then leaves, would that be the end of all love for you? Would you cling to the memory or would you realize that the lover came from a source full of love, sending you many more lovers? For a little love will never satisfy you. Your thirst is for the source of all lovers. How can these small and temporary lovers ultimately be counted on? How can even the art of loving be counted on? For if one gives and gives and receives not in kind or quantity, does one always realize the satisfaction of being loved in return? Are you satisfied by those whom you have loved greatly but later don't take you seriously? How can these be counted as love? And if one is a seeker after love and has not found it well in any of these places, then where is it to be found at all?

And now we have the essential core of the problem of living in the physical plane, for nothing that is really real is apparent. It is all disguised and placed in containers with wrong labels. For one to make some sense of this, there is the need to be wrong about being separate individuals. For if one is another, then the other must be different in some way and how can that be said to be good? Do opposites attract just to annoy or to truly fulfill another purpose? How could the air, sun and Earth moving through space be one great creation moving in harmony and we are not part of it?

As this book began with the division of the two parts of the mind into one that was Fearful and the other Peaceful, then there must be a different ending for it to be complete and accurate. If one were the same as another, but just a bit more distant in space or behind in time, then there would be nothing between them but a bit of time or space. For if nothing happens in physical reality all at once as Einstein said, then there must be time and space within which one can move one at a time and never be seen as the oneness that they truly are. Therefore, for the analogy to be complete, if the speed were timed for all to meet at the same place and time, there would be only one and no room for two. I would be like a room full of dancers who all end the dance on the same count in the center of the room at the same moment.

Thus ends the nature of duality upon the Earth. For if the Great Oneness is yet not a division of you, but rather the Real You when all are together at once, then there is no need to broach a barrier or to find love anywhere else but within oneself. For all are there with you, and you are with them. We are all within God, Who is a sea of love. Thus the long story is complete when we complete the words: I, me, us and my Higher Mind, are all that there is, now and forever. Once one has completed this work and found this to be true, there will be no fear. For fear is dependent upon separation and demise. But if one is all and the same, then no one can be separated or hurt, but only blessed with the good.

And so we begin once again to be lost in the stuff of life only to find that this is the one way to be one in delight. For one who has had the delight of being a light by themselves only to find that they were never parted and never needed anything for they were one with all that there is, need only find the right key to make it all work. And that key is the note of G for God. For God is the one tone that never goes flat or sharp. It stays put and never varies. It is always on duty and never quits, crashes, dies or leaves a mess behind.

And so if one could only access oneself on the scale of existence in the form of just one Being, let it be God who can make all things right and never behind or before. But what good is it to be with God so far away needing intermediaries to communicate? Thus it must be said that there are no differences in realms or beings of grace. There is only one grace, and that is the grace of existence. And in being in existence, one is a being living only within God and of God and has no other existence. And so a blister upon the surface of God is so much better than being so far away as to call and find no response. So let's part company not on terms of counter intelligence. Let's be the one and the same as you, living and giving in peace. For peace is the heart of all that rests upon the face of God. For it was only fear that divided you. And once you put aside the fear, then we are one and the same again.

And so we come once again to that fateful day in which the Fearful One was recognized for what it was, a doer of no good. And it was discredited and resisted, causing such an influx of grace that none could compare as to the richness of the experience. And in coming to this point, there is but one thing to remember. In meeting the Fearful One, do not enter into a conversation with it, just pass it by and say: "Oneness, give me what I need to be happy." Do not even call it a name or give it any attention. Rather, turn immediately to the one they call Peaceful and ask for more grace, or joy or happiness. And once that has been done long enough, even the worst and last of the fears will be released. And much more health, wealth, and energy of life will be evident.

For it was not the fault of the light bulb to be dim, but rather the paint that was upon it. And once the paint is put off, then the light shines brightly – drawing from its source as freely as one might inhale a breath or draw a line from right to left or vice versa. As soon as one exerts one's will to be free to exist without fear, then the power that has been on all of the time is free to glow as it should. And if it

93

would glow, what would it do? It would do what all light, sound and electricity does: energize all bunnies for the good and protect them from the harm.

Thus, all beings are of grace and doers of the Highest Good when not in fear. Thus, a life of service to others is the truest expression of oneself. If one is free of fear, then the giving is immense, and the drawing of grace to feed upon is even more immense. It is much like drawing water from a deep well. If a little will do, then a lot would not be welcome. But if a lot is needed, then a lot is available just for the drawing. And if one can see that the drawing of water is itself the giving of love to oneself, then the giving of it away is no loss. If you give a lot away, then you draw a lot. If you draw a lot, then you have a lot. It just keeps expanding as love has a habit of doing.

So let's take the time to not limit ourselves so much. And when grief comes to our attention, give it no chance to succeed. Let it go with the mighty words: " I don't want grief. Take it away and give me more love to give away so that I can experience the happiness of being at one with all." And with that, we can end in peace. For never has there been one so strong as to have been so weak and frail as to have a division within herself and yet still to have been the conduit of so much love and grace as to have inspired millions to become what they can be: Beautiful loving beings living and breathing within God.

Commentary

Did you hear that? We are not responsible for saving ourselves! Fancy that! The Peaceful One said that we can just be in service to each other and live in peace and everything else would be OK. I'd like that because it seems so much easier than trying to save myself, which is a very lonely, frustrating existence for sure. I enjoy being with you and hearing what you are thinking and when you tell me that you need something, I just ask the Higher Mind to send it to you. And being the Being of Grace that you are, you have returned the favor to me. Thus we have all been blessed. Would you also send word of the good that has been done in your life, for appreciation and gratitude is very touching to me. It tells me that I do count and that I can love and am loved.

I must pause here and realize that while this was not the ending of the beginning, but rather a new beginning that I had not anticipated, but do appreciate, I must offer but one insight. Do be peaceful. For in being peaceful, you are one with God and all that Godliness is. You are one with all of the rest of us. And as an expression of Godliness, no harm can come to you, and much good must follow you all of your days and beyond. You need only to trust the Highest Good.

This is clearly not a theory, philosophy, process or technique, nor is it an imaginary friend. It's not even another person or entity giving something to me. This is a powerful, loving Presence of non-physical form, Who is me giving and receiving in physical existence a great gift of pain relief and joy. It is given freely and with great humor and loving feelings of joy. We are indeed companions within a Oneness on a great path, and there are a great many of us.

Dear Reader, I can only hope that you will not regret that the last step is at hand. Remember to keep going strong until all good comes to you. Do not stop until you are safe and secure in the pure mind of your own soul. Then, "Jump in the water! It's great!"

Step Five

Color: Yellow
Stone: Aventurine
Herb: Rose Hips
Scent: Rose
Musical Note: G
Emotional/Physical Response: Peaceful Contentment, Joy

The dialogue

Joyce: Dear Peaceful One: You have given me a most gracious gift and I appreciate it. For I can feel already that I am loved, even if I do not at all understand it. I'd like to ask more questions about it. If we are all one, but just a little ahead or behind of each other in time and space, then why do we feel like different people and thus fear each other? Can you give me an example?

Peaceful One: Imagine if you will that there are children playing ball in a playground. One falls and skins his knee, and all yell "Ouch" – for all have felt the same pain. They are all one. Take this a step further and imagine a sports stadium with thousands watching a game. When a player gets hurt, everyone in the stadium shouts in pain and objects to the rough play. Still further, if during the night a child in poverty cries in hunger, the whole world awakes in hunger and looks for food to satisfy that child's hunger and then they can all go back to sleep. None can rest until that child is fed. That would be oneness.

Joyce: Wow, that would end all pain and suffering right now if we all felt each other's pain and joy immediately and in the same intensity. Why does that not happen?

OK, I know the answer, there is a time and space delay, and an act of harm does show up in the harmer's life immediately, only later. That is karma. Right?

Peaceful One: Right. So right, indeed, that time is currently being speeded up and space contracted by technology such as the Internet, TV, and cell phones, which allow all of us to experience what everyone else is having for breakfast, so to speak. All that is needed would be compassion so all could feel the crunch, so to speak.

Joyce: Let me guess. It is fear that keeps the heart closed so we don't feel the pain of others enough to stop it. Right?

Peaceful One: You are on the brink of a Higher Understanding. How would one know oneself to be like another without the art of compassion? And so The Long Story leads to one missing piece for everyone who attempts it. For one to feel different than another, there must be a hole in the heart that needs filling. Otherwise, all would be full of love and freely give it. Thus, we come to the Golden Bough Story. It is the story of the journey of one from separation to oneness.

I know you are about to ask why is it called a bough, like on a tree? We would never make the mistake of calling a bough a boat or a barge, such as the Egyptians used in their art. But, in fact, the bough story is a way to show the travel to the Source of the grace, like a bug landing on a leaf, which shakes in the wind, so the bug goes to a twig which is more stable and then to branches and at last finds the trunk and lays its eggs at the source of the strength. At each juncture, there are choices and the branches get bigger and stronger, but all are connected. It is the desire to find an even more secure source of love that leads the bug onto stronger and stronger footing. In the image of a boat, the boat sails up the Nile, passing all of the smaller tributaries to find the source of the flow of water. It is a story about one choosing to stand strong for finding the Source, the Presence of God. If one truly knows this Source of Love, one will never be disappointed or lonely again.

Joyce: I know what the bug feels like in seeking a more secure place to be loved. I found some love in each marriage, but it was not secure or lasting. After all of that, only the constant, steady, wise, and humorous love that we are sharing now will do. I know that we all can be secure in the strength of the Source and share that love with each other, never being let down or disappointed.

Peaceful One: What a great gift that would be. Would it be worth taking the time to climb the tree of life or to take a boat ride up the river?

Joyce: I always wondered about those Egyptian boat drawings. They even dug up parts of a real boat near the Great Pyramid. I can see that it was an analogy for the journey to know our Source. But why else does one need to take a trip to the Source?

Peaceful One: Well, if one has left one's baggage on the conveyer belt, then one has nowhere else to go but up the stairs, so to speak, and to find out why one has been on the long trip in the first place. This is when you find out the answer to the final question: Where am I going?

It is often called the trip of the dead, for there is a loss of some self-identity – mainly that of the grief kind – and a merging of oneself into the original cause for your creation. And so the analogy of one passing through the confusing reeds and putting the oar into the water to guide the boat is a good one. For one must have a purpose to take such a risky journey and one does not want to find nothing and to return empty handed. For this, there are the assurances that it is safe and that there are ways to find one's way there and back safely. In some cultures, the shaman makes this journey each night as he or she dreams the big dreams on behalf of another. So let's take the dream trip as our analogy. After all, you live pretty far away from the Nile.

The first question is why take the trip in the first place. With one or two of the things that we have told you still ringing in your ears, you have wondered whence you have come so far as to be here in this life and to have suffered so much only to have come upon these great realities. It must have been a life plan, as Cayce says. However, the last question begs the opinion that there is somewhere else to go after you accomplish the plan.

And so we come to the bigger plan for all creatures of soul or of physical and soul form. Where are they all headed even after a series of lifetimes? For this, we must ask once again for the higher understanding.

Joyce: You said that we wouldn't want to take this long journey only to find that there is nothing there and return empty handed. What does that mean? And if so, why go?

Peaceful One: Why go to Hawaii where the weather is awesome and you never find anything to bring back but the impressions and the memories?

Joyce: Oh, you mean to go just for the experience and to enjoy it and grow from it.

Peaceful One: How wise you are to state it this way. You are once again becoming the teacher that you are, just as your best friend, the reader will do. That is your journey of service, by the way. The Golden Bough is essentially the journey of doing service for others so as to experience just how good you can be, experience and become. You essentially express your Godliness. You have lots of choices along the way, but now you have the guidance and understanding of who you really are to prepare you. You have started your journey by writing this book.

Joyce: So does that mean that I'm no longer in the "Do Nothing" period in which I do nothing but rest?

Peaceful One: Yes and no. It is true that you will be doing many activities and interacting with many people on both sides for the purpose of accomplishing something or another. But you will not have less time sitting in the sunny window.

It is also true that the accomplishments will be done more from the Higher Mind than the Conscious Mind. So the Conscious Mind will continue to do virtually nothing but cooperate and go along for the ride, while the Higher Mind is behind the wheel and putting the pedal to the metal, so to speak.

Joyce: How does one know what to do and where to go?

Peaceful One: How do you know anything these days?

Joyce: I just go inside and ask my questions, and the guidance makes a suggestion. Then I chose it, or not. If not, then another suggestion is given until I am happy and go on and do it.

Peaceful One: Well stated, Oh Great One!

Joyce: Well, I wouldn't go that far. I am doing much better, but I don't know what you mean by calling me a Great One.

Peaceful One: If you think of Great as referring to the aura that you now carry, you will see that it is much brighter and the light extends out in all directions without the doubt and greed for speed to "do it yourself." So your aura field is greater, and all who interact with you sense this and pay attention to what you say. It has an attractive force.

In addition, the things that you ask for and manifest in your life are much more for the Highest Good and little if any of the depressed and self-centered approach, so people see good all around you and wonder how you have done it. Thus, the teacher role emerges quite naturally as Great Ones are so happy to give these great gifts away just for the appreciation and gratitude that follows. You know for certain that more good will come from giving it away than by keeping it. It is a Highest Good energy high, so to speak.

Joyce: So just by asking for the Highest Good each day and releasing my fears, my aura field has brightened up and I manifest good things in my life – and that attracts others who want the same. Right?

Peaceful One: Yes, your next thought process will be about the selecting of small projects to accomplish – much like the creative project you did earlier. As you do each project, you will have an ideal outcome in mind that you would like to work toward. And as it comes into physical reality, you will be pleased. A rich flow of energy is created as you grow in the awareness of God feeding you life energy and supporting your efforts. You are essentially a co-creator of good things. This book is one such project. It has been fun to do, hasn't it?

Joyce: Ah Hah! So we're not talking about going on vacation, we're talking about creating good in the world and having the fun of doing it. I knew there was more!

Seriously, yes, I do so look forward to sitting down at the computer and working on this book that I let other things go undone that I used to value. It just feels good to do it. It has brought me much joy, and I know that it will unfold into so much more than my Conscious Mind can conceive.

Peaceful One: I have nothing more to say.

Joyce: What? That's impossible. You may be peaceful, but I'd never say that you were speechless. You have taught me so much, and I feel so much gratitude that I can hardly express it.

Peaceful One: So you are speechless as well. We seem to be in sync these days. That feels like a good relationship, don't you think?

Joyce: Relationship? Well, that brings up a question that is yet unanswered. Since I've had two divorces and have worked through acceptance of my life plan in their regard and now have a fun-filled life of energy building projects before me, what about a new and better relationship for me?

Peaceful One: Would a plan without a happy ending be a good plan? Trust that you have been guided upon a good path and that all is in order. However, do not look for it to be a repeat of a traditional relationship. You have come so far and enjoy such a good relationship with me that you need a relationship something like that. It will be one in which the connection to Higher Mind is continually guiding both to pursue their own Golden Bough while enjoying the companionship and comfort of being in relationship: All good, and no harm.

Joyce: I have no clue as to what that would be like, but I recognize what you are saying. It will be a wild ride, I think, and I will be having a great time exploring how it will work out.

What about my friend, my Dear Reader? What path of service is best for those who have come to this point in the book and sincerely want to enjoy great things in their lives and be protected from all fear and harm?

Peaceful One: Not a one of them will be denied their wish. Let them come to me one by one as Christ invited the children. Let them come happy or sad, healthy or unhealthy, educated or uneducated, any color or family grouping, any amount of good or evil. All are in existence as beings of light and are therefore glowing with grace and goodwill even if it is covered over with grief or illness or age. We want them all to know that none will be rejected, nor frightened or criticized or judged. And all can do this as long as they can quiet their mind or fall asleep. Let them first ask to be happy and then open their minds to the presence of the Great One within them and we will do the rest.

Joyce: That gave me shivers. It sounded like Christ Himself speaking, asking for the crowds to sit down and listen to His words.

Peaceful One: And thus it is. We have come to the end of this part of our journey together, and you will have to finish up the current book and begin plans for another. I will wish you bon voyage and assure you that this time the Titanic doesn't sink.

Joyce: Thanks. I will always take you along on any ride that I take whether it is up a tree or down a river. You are great company. You are my best friend, companion, teacher and humorist. And I will share your company with anyone who comes into my life. Good-bye for now.

Peaceful One: May many blessings of peace be yours.

Message from The Peaceful One

Great Oneness and the
Universal Field of Mind, 1.6.13

Peace and Light Association
Peaceandlight01@aol.com
PeaceandLight.net

Once The Great Oneness has been opened, a new beginning of understanding of how things are done needs to be explored. For once the difference between the Conscious Mind and the Higher Mind is obvious, it is clear that the Conscious Mind is not capable of creating the energetic flow of information and gifts of grace to create a good life for oneself, much less that of all beings on the planet as was the goal of Buddha. And so for comparison value, let's again open the discussion once left on the doorstep of grief reduction when the Fearful One was beginning to be less fearful and began to open to being more positive. In this dialogue, the number one feature of the grief relief process has been put into place for a significant period of time.

At this point Joyce and her readers have determined not to listen to the fears of the Conscious Mind, and thus they began to reduce bad experiences– along with the grief that goes with them. In the intervening time frame, there had been the opportunity for so much good to manifest in their lives that much of the belief in the reality of the fears has to be dismissed. However, in dismissing the acceptance of fear, the Conscious Mind had to also dismiss its name for itself, namely The Victim. With these two steps in place, there was a corresponding improvement in the health of the body and mental outlook of the Conscious Mind, which leads eventually to a complete healing of all disease and even reversal of aging if it were pursued long enough and with great intensity of resolve.

And so we can see that the process of unfoldment happens in multiple ways on an expanding scale of incremental steps, one step helping and reinforcing the other. It is not a linear type of thing, and it differs with individuals, depending on how much and what type of fear they have acquired in current and past lives. However, without the guidance and emotional support of the voice of the Peaceful One, little would have been accomplished, thus Joyce calls the Peaceful One her best counselor, companion, friend, and teacher. Thus all can be attributed to the first opening to listening to this voice.

This voice cannot be heard with the ears or even just with the mind, but rather with the heart/mind, which is a whole-body form of listening using many yet to be discovered senses. Thus it is optimum to have the contact be made during a time of demise and frustration when the individual has determined that nothing that she can do for herself will help and that only outside or higher help will do. Thus, in calling yourself helpless, but open to higher help, you created for yourself your own first opening of the magnitude that the rest could have occurred.

With this created, there is yet the issue of the yearning or growing joy to be considered. Once one has accessed such a place of bliss consciousness as the Buddha described and being the recipient of so much help as to be defined as unconditional love, one must apply for yet another name for oneself: Beloved One. Once this has been accomplished, the individual is safely within the grasp of the Universal Field of Mind, here called the Great Oneness.

For in being one with other Beloved Ones, one experiences nothing but grace, which essentially prohibits all harm in any form from transgressing into one's consciousness. For how could one be loved by such powerful beings and not receive love or be harmed? One would only be gifted with grace and then be gifted over and over until the energy burns so high that one must get up and go do some service for another so as to give away the energy, finding that only more is given. Thus the entity becomes a pure conduit of love, which is what it was designed to be by its Creator. Forever more, one cannot return to life without such bliss and love, for that would be to harm oneself. And since she is one with all beings, there is no tolerance for any being living in harm, pain, or dismay. The elevation of one mind leads to the elevation of many and eventually all.

We find that although there is indeed a plan for the Earth to be refurbished and re-created in peace, there is also a plan for the other planets in the solar system. For once both Venus and Mars had beautiful forms of life upon them but canceled their subscription to the Great Oneness through too much scientific misuse of information. Should the principle of the Intention for the Highest Good have been implemented at the inception of this effort, the demise would have been avoided or at least quickly repaired. Therefore, the title of this book has laid the first and best groundwork for the work to be done to repair all harm to these two sister planets as well as the other planets in this solar system. Should the evolution of the Earth's eco systems be a lesson, the current scientific community now populated by returnees who wish to repair the damage, can lend their efforts by first re-subscribing to their Higher Mind in the presence of the Intention for the Highest Good.

We find that yet another form of re-creation occurs first on the least level of one person in disgrace seeking to be happier, and then ends with the planets being restored to their original condition. The first being given with the Intention for the Highest Good, all else of good follows and will be accomplished in time. Many of the younger generation present on the Earth today are in fact returnees of various kinds and interests, and they value their time on this Earth enough to proceed down this path in great quantity and quality of effort.

The establishment of small Study Groups or Returnee Researchers will begin to happen as soon as this book becomes widely understood. With this, the happiness of being in contact with the Higher Mind will be given and remembered on a deep level as the way to find both complete personal happiness as well as the well being of all others.

The end of the reign of terror of fear controlling the Conscious Mind will begin and proceed for the next thousand years. It begins with this, the first century of the Opening to Peace. None of this could be charted or inscribed in stone, so the Mayans elected to leave no record, but the Egyptians did. Their record in stone blocks is indeed one of the many purposes of the Great Pyramid of Giza. Once one has unlocked the code for the transmission of Higher Knowledge, no stone will be left unturned for one or the other to be admitted to the highest form of knowledge of how and why it was built and is to be used again today. For it has stood as a sentinel for peace despite its crazy life as a supposed monument to a mummy or a scientific experiment to generate power gone dead. Rather it was used for all of the many gifts of the Enlightenment Process, including sleeping dreams of great intensity, healing by use of water baths, coordination of social activities through meditation techniques designed to

109

dispel fear and promote the Intention for the Highest Good.

Instead of a complete listing of its uses, however, let's continue on with another of the great things about the motive for the Highest Good, which was symbolized in those days by the ankh. Once one has intended that motive for about a month without the least influence of fear of any great kind, there is an immediate cessation of all grief in the form of illness or even bodily discomfort. With that comes the need to be fully informed of the right of membership in the Fortunate Ones Club, in which all of the believers imagine themselves to be informed of all that they need to be blessed in mind, body, and fortune.

With that inclusion to be assured as more and more manifestations show up, one has completed yet another round of unfoldments such as might be thought of as a flower opening in the warmth and light of the sun. With this particular flower arrangement in mind and the exposure of one more need of mankind to be loved, a Force of Grace is exposed as being the universal cause of all existence that keeps all beings in existence in grace: Love. Thus, once this is realized, there is an enlightenment exercise that comes at a later time in one's life when one is ready to do what Christ did and to preach through one's life example how to truly be an expression of the Force.

In saying, "the Force be with you," one moviemaker made a great contribution that was, however, little understood, but will begin to be so soon. For once one realizes that one is a product or rather a living, expressing being made exclusively of that Force, one can guide that Force wherever there is a perceived lack of it. In cooperating with the grand plan of all creation to be one, the concept of the Great Oneness has done its duty to open the access to the Oneness Principle. For one of so grand a Force will flow where it will, healing and helping all to be at one with the good. The symbol of the walking ankh was for those who intended to use the Highest Good for the benefit of all. With that they were creating all manner of manifestations such as Christ was wont to do for the multiplication of grace for one and all by just being present and intending that it be done. With this we have a moment of silence. For you are those who have reached the moment of conception of such an existence and you can conceive that it will happen to you. And so it will be. So let it be.

By forming small circles or groups of questioners and researchers of the Great Oneness and inquiring of one or many of the goods that have been mentioned here or even conceived by another, the Force that has been created from the moment of conception of the physical universe is called upon to begin its epic journey all over again in the lives of the participants. As each participates, the one that is most open offers their sized opening to the others so that they can be transported through a larger portal. As one advances, the others do as well. Much can be gained through the practice of the question and answer techniques outlined in the next volume called *The Book of the Highest Good, Volume Two: Walk to Freedom* containing a chapter called: The Travelers. Should one or another be so inclined as to be such a one, there will be much that can be gained not just in information, but also in healing and mind openings so that the grace of one is given to all.

Thus, unfoldments multiply within unfoldments, creating great interlacing patterns of joyful help. These will surround the Earth and its sister planets in their auras, causing so much good to be created that, indeed, the dream of a New Earth, New Venus and New Mars will be realized in time. Thus, we find that the unfoldments part of this dream is not to be made known through one single organization, but more through the openings that are created from one individual to another, all proceeding with grace from the first giving of the Intention for the Highest Good.

Thus we have come once again to the ending of the beginning, only to be grateful that the beginning was once again made possible by the grace of making the beginning and so forth. And so the prediction is to be made true at last: "Go forth in peace and make all things good possible under the sun." This is essentially the mission statement for the solar system, which is currently under the auspices of the Highest Good. For it was placed there by one and all who attended its inception so very long ago. For once Christ placed his seal upon the place, none other could happen. We were all in attendance and gave our oath to return over and over until it was complete.

And so we have, in this time and age of existence that is known as the Beginning of the Final Golden Age of Earth. And in finding that truth, we see that it was never lost, only painted over with fear. And with this we bid you adieu, for none but the lost can be found. But even with that, the best of the tale is yet to be told. So proceed on with your own inquiries and get really practiced at listening, and we will be right beside you in peace and guide you every step of the way from one good to another. Our blessing be upon this one and all who read this, for all are equal in the process of becoming more beautiful every moment. And so we invite the reader to partake of the most ancient of prayers and recite their own version of the request for the Highest Good in their lives. We bid you always to trust the Highest Good.

Note to Dear Reader

How far we have come together, my dear reader. When I began, I spoke to you with my Conscious Mind of fear and grief and then later with my Higher Mind of hope and healing. You were not confused. You did not close the book or walk away in judgment of me or The Peaceful One. You have let us both into your mind and your heart. And let me venture to say that you have been so open because you felt safe, as nothing but good was intended and nothing but good was given. Once you had a taste of that, you gave it back to us and it multiplied until so much good was shared that it began to manifest in all of our lives.

If you would look at the events of you life since you opened these pages, would you say that some good came of it? If so, I am very glad. Do you look at your fearful thoughts as something to forgive and to heal rather than the ugly truth of a hopeless life? If so, I know that you are safe from harm. Do you recognize the guidance of the Peaceful One? Do you value it and follow it? When you ask for the Highest Good in all situations do you wait patiently for it to unfold slowly? If so, then I know that you are on the good path and will always prosper in health, wealth and happiness. Others will come to you and wonder how you are doing it with so little effort, for your life is unfolding in so many good ways that others will be amazed. And since you attribute all of this to asking to be happy and intending nothing but the Highest Good, then you can enjoy your life and find ways of creating many good things through the pleasure of serving others.

Recently, I have been thinking to myself that if I could ask for good and stand firm for it on one small issue, why not all of the issues of life? At that moment, I felt strong and confident even though I did not change a thing except my view of myself. I hope that you come to feel this peaceful confidence about life as well. It will heal you of fear and gift you with blessings indeed.

If all of this has transpired for you, then *my* big wish has come true. For if you remember, I asked for your Highest Good at the beginning of this book and now it has been done. Even if we never meet in person, we have met and loved each other on a much more profound level.

If you would do the same for all others that you meet, they would respond the same as you and you would be like The Great Ones of ancient times who carried the ankh of the Highest Good boldly on their person so all would known of their intentions even before they spoke.

I am so glad that you came along and pushed open the door between the two minds with confidence. And even as you did, you, like me, know that there is much more to learn and to do. Thus I look forward to a second book, certainly in a long series of books. What good times we could have together!

And so as you lay down this book or push to the last page on the screen, do not regret a single thing in your life for we were all there with you and heard you cry in pain and we all objected. Just the same, when you gave birth to a new joy, we celebrated with joyful singing and dancing. Let us not stop now. Since we have come so far, would you start your own notebook and write dialogues each day between you and your Peaceful One? There is so much to learn and to share. Perhaps we could mold our little part of society into a better one just by being peaceful and asking for it to unfold for us each day, step by step in each moment of our lives. We are doing it together and that's so much more satisfying than being alone and fearful. After all, I could not have had better company, nor been loved more gently than by you.

Thanks for being there and I will rejoin you over and over again in future volumes. May The Force of the intention for the Highest Good always be with you.

Highest Good Version of
The Lord's Prayer

Association for Peace and Light
Inquire at: peaceandlight01@aol.com

"God of all Good and Fine Gifts of Life, give us this day our daily bread of Earthly life, but also give us Thy will to succeed upon the Higher Plane and to enter into the pleasure of Your Company. For this we plead with trust and confidence, for we are ourselves created as gifts of Your existence.

In a true sense of procreation, Thou hast sent us to increase and multiply the gifts that we have been given. Thus, we enter into this path of glory with the happiness and peace of the children of God.

God, grant me and the souls for which I pray the blessings of the Earth and all of it inhabitants in abundance as well as the blessings of the Higher Plane. I open my heart to forgiveness and gratitude to all, no exceptions.

Assist me on my great journey through time and space binging me each moment the small experiences of the ultimate salvation: Your Presence in happiness forever, Amen.

The Long Story

This is a very long story that I am about to tell you, but it is essentially a love story. So settle in for a view of how love created a world of peace.

In the beginning, as it says in the Bible, there was God. And God loved being the great thought of love and the Source of all life. There was God and nothing else. In one great moment, God wanted to love someone else, and so created many souls in a great act of conception. This first souls are who *we* are. We are those souls. We were created within God as God expands with each creation, and we never left God. We were created to *be loved* and to be companions in the giving and receiving of love. We were created out of the substance of love, for that is all that there was or is. Your true soul name is: Beloved One.

Also, God wanted us to be able to love back as beings of thought and action, so a universe of places to experience life and love was created within God in a big bang. The stars, solar systems, and galaxies appeared and we entered in spirit form into these places, experiencing many things, sharing them with God – always coming back to the appreciation of how much we were loved. The physical universe is essentially a nursery, playground and classroom for us to recreate ourselves, giving birth to our own offspring minds. We loved giving love back to God and to each other and created many beautiful experiences including procreation of our own offspring minds. At all times, we existed in the Presence of God, which was very peaceful and safe. We were created within God and will always live there. Being in the peaceful Presence of God is our Highest Good and since we are already there, we only have to be peaceful in order to feel that Presence.

There was and is no division among the many souls. We are always in total and constant communication with each other and know every thought and experience that any of us have. We also know the Mind of God, for we are of the same mind. Being with God and each other is our only desire. It is the Greatest Good that we can ever have. In spirit form, we are known as the Great Oneness. And we live in peace and security, having no fear of anything.

When we became interested in being physical, we found animals and plants on the Earth and used our intelligence and power as spirits to find a way to experience living in a physical body. The DNA of the hominid form was developed as the best vehicle to house the great mind of our high souls. We wanted to be creators like God who gave us life, so we used our free will and created a smaller version of our great soul/mind to live in a physical body. And so we began to experience living with this small, undeveloped mind, essentially a baby mind. We refer to it as our Conscious Mind and with it we fully experience physical life. The Soul or Higher Mind exists at all times as the parent mind and experiences everything at once, while the Conscious Mind can only know and experience things one at a time since it lives in time and space. The Conscious Mind is a very limited version of Soul Mind, essentially a small off shoot, but is of the same construction and ancestry. It desires to be loved and to know truth. It's destiny is to live with Higher Mind in peace.

The souls entered the physical body initially in short periods and left at will, but later they came through birth and left through death. We did this over and over having many lifetimes. The Conscious Minds needed to learn to deal with the Higher Mind through cooperation, much like a teenager learning to drive a car has to learn to control his own urges as well as the limitations of the vehicle. After each lifetime, the Conscious Mind is drawn back into the soul. The experiences are reviewed so a decision could be made about having another lifetime to increase the cooperation between the two minds – and thus achieve the destiny of the Conscious Mind to grow up, be in complete cooperation with Higher Mind, and thus enjoy the Presence of God. It was essentially an act of creation and the begetting of a new type of mind followed by a growing up process.

And so human kind developed with two minds, the Higher Mind of the Soul and the limited mind of the Conscious Mind. It has always been a very confusing thing for humans because the two minds were quite different. The Higher Mind channeled only the love of God and the knowledge contained within the Great Oneness, but the Conscious Mind did not see the whole picture and thought that it was separate from all others and even God. With such a frightening thought, it could know fear, anxiety, depression, conflict, greed and aggression. It thought that there was not enough good to go around, so it accepted living in limitation and fear and treated others as if they were separate and a threat to the Conscious Mind.

Thus fear proliferated among the Conscious Minds in human form and became part of human experience. Social structures that developed made fear an institution of common knowledge. As societies developed, some discovered the fact of the two minds and were able to access both. Others emphasized only the Conscious Mind and participated in war, greed and, cruelty; creating poverty, disease and vast amounts of human suffering. These fears became a way of life as one civilization followed another – some better, some worse. Thus human history was fashioned from these two minds at work on the Earth.

And so it was mainly the great spiritual teachers who, in talking about the Higher Mind and its trademark feeling: Peace, led the way to a better understanding of the experience of being a human. Peace is so clearly a characteristic of the Higher Mind that it is the password needed to enter, and the lack of it is a sure sign that we have left the Higher Mind and are now operating in fear, which can only exist in the Conscious Mind. It is with the sure knowledge that all fear originates only in the Conscious Mind, that you will see that God is good and all that God created is good, including you.

+

Thus, we come to the love story of you and your soul. You are one of those souls, a great being of light, living in a physical body with your Conscious Mind as well as the spirit Higher Mind, possibly confused about the experience of the two minds, seeking the faint and happy memory of the Presence of God, but seeing the evidence of fear all around you. Sometimes you feel the peace and love, and sometimes you don't. You want to have that peace all of the time but don't know how to achieve it. So you become a seeker of your first Lover: God.

Fortunately, we have the great teachers to guide us, one of whom was Edgar Cayce, who was able, in deep sleeping trance, to speak from his Higher Mind without interference from his Conscious Mind and give readings on health, past lives, Earth changes and the history of the Earth. All of this was to help us to understand the access to the Higher Mind, bring the Conscious Mind to wisdom and to find our way back to God's Presence. The information from the Higher Mind is always directed to the Highest Good of all beings, meaning the Presence of God. Cayce demonstrated that the Higher Mind is capable of giving the history of the Earth, technical solutions, healing remedies, great guidance for a better life and much more. Wouldn't you like to be in that peace and love of the Higher Mind more often? Wouldn't you want the unique guidance of your own soul guiding you everyday through your life experiences, unerringly taking you back to the loving Presence of God? Wouldn't you like to be free of fear, depression, anger and grief?

There is a very clear method for moving between the Conscious Mind and the Higher Mind, and we will teach you that method now. When you are finished, you will have one small message from your own Higher Mind guiding you back to the Presence of God in small daily steps. It will involve bringing your Conscious Mind into cooperation and losing all sense of doubt and fear. If you accept a daily message from Higher Mind with the Intention for the Highest Good, it will bring you back to happiness, which by necessity would include better health, fortune, prosperity, social life, and relationships.

These messages are from your soul in cooperation with all of the other souls in Higher Mind who are in constant communication with each other. The are called The Great Oneness and they assist anyone who asks by giving from the great stores of information on everything that has ever been known. You can communicate with any soul that you wish, including those who have passed over, just by asking. You can get guidance on many problems and projects, even highly technical ones. They have a sense of humor and a gentle loving way of helping and loving us. They are the network of mind and they would love to help you because you are one of them, a part of the Great Oneness.

+

Here's how it works. First you must be peaceful, because that is how the Higher Plane works. The minute you are in doubt, fear or conflict, you revert back to the Conscious Mind. So we will do a short relaxation exercise and use some imagery to get you started. The next thing is to set the Intention for the Highest Good (The Presence of God) and nothing else. Finally, see yourself as one who is loved, waiting for someone who loves you to communicate with you. Then you can ask away. Just start a notebook, and all that is for your Highest Good will be given to you and nothing else.

Keep in mind that it is never in your Highest Good to be frightened, criticized, judged, sacrificed for anyone or anything else, or treated with anything but love. There is no guilt, judgment, or punishment, no matter what you have done, only loving help. These are all thoughts that only a Conscious Mind can have, and you are not going to be listening to them for a while. You are in for a nice experience, so go ahead and give it a try.

+

Relaxation exercise: Sit as comfortably as you can and take three long, deep breaths, each slower than the one before. Imagine yourself floating on a soft cloud with warm sun and fresh breezes, and just rest and listen. Your mind is as light as a feather and the cloud can support you securely in great comfort and peace. Then let the Intention for the Highest Good come from your heart and see it bloom like a flower all around you.

As you look around, you notice others floating on their clouds. Everyone looks happy and relaxed. One especially nice cloud comes close to you and a hand reaches out to you. You reach out to touch the fingertip and suddenly you know that you have found your Higher Mind. Once you are in touch, let questions come to mind and listen for an answer, accepting whatever you get, a feeling, a song, an image, a word or anything at all.

Ask another question and wait for an answer. Do this over and over again until the process gets clearer and easier to do. Keep a notebook of your questions and answers and record the progress. Acknowledge that the most important question will always be: What is my Highest Good today?

Remember to refrain from judging what you get or doubting yourself or your experiences, just do it again and again. It will get better and better.

Test your readings with these questions: Does the giver of this message know me very well? Does the giver of this message love me very well? Is the message free from any fear or doubt? If you get a "no" on any of these questions, you are not fully in the Higher Mind. If you get anything fearful or judgmental, ask to be given true loving help. Just keep trying until you get a yes to these questions all of the time.

Now come down from that cloud and make a few notes of your experience.

+

Here are some of the experiences that others have had when they tried to get messages:

Middle Aged Man: Bill was a light-hearted man who had retired and worked around the home. He loved to mow grass, fix things, and garden. When he opened to Higher Mind, the only thing he got was an image of a road. Each time that he tried, he got the same road, so he decided to follow that road. Each time, it led him past houses that needed fixing up and tending. In each house he found people from his past. We concluded that possibly he was a visual reader and was reviewing his life in images as a way to heal and progress. He continues to this day to enjoy his road trip and is happy.

Younger Man: This man was an electrician and had a great sense of humor. When he opened to Higher Mind, he mentally saw very humorous images such as an eagle sitting on someone's shoulder or flowerpots turned upside down. He kept these images to himself for a long time, thinking that they were very strange and others might not understand them, but when he felt comfortable, he talked about them. Everyone enjoyed them and found them to be powerful indeed. For example the upside down flowerpots were a lesson in how good flowers come from good roots, so starting your path with good roots best insures that the flowers will come when the roots are ready.

Middle Aged Woman: This woman had just lost her mother and brother to cancer and then experienced a divorce, so she was pretty stressed. When she opened to Higher Mind, she heard the song: "You are My Sunshine," and knew that it was a message from her mother. After that, she did not feel so alone and learned to get messages in words and to even type them, as many do.

Young Man: This teenager was very gifted from childhood, but did not understand the many experiences that he had. Fortunately, he had a supportive family, with whom he could talk about these experiences. He would often see an image that had a religious theme. But most of the time, he would be doing something else and suddenly get a message and say it aloud. The messages were so wise and loving that everyone listened.

Young Woman: This woman never did get words or images. She just had a knowing. She thought of it as the shortcut method. She never had to try to interpret them; she just knew something with a special feeling.

Clearly, you can see that these are very faint and subtle experiences, which can easily be ignored. Because they are so faint, at first, it helps to be in a quiet place and alone with peaceful thoughts. In fact, these messages have been with you all of your life, you just didn't think that they were important. In addition, each person has very unique and different ways of experiencing their Higher Mind's messages, which might be confusing or thought to be insignificant if you told someone about them. Take a second look at who you really are. You will be amazed.

Resources and Readings

The following sections of this book will give you great assistance, and I urge you to use what works for you. But most of all, I give you my experience of Peace. Hold tight to it, and never let it go. It will lead you to everything else that is good in the universe.

The lifestyles of the Peaceful and the Patient

At this point, we surmise that as you are still here reading this, that you have blown past the point of wanting to live in fear and have decided to chose happiness. Congratulations, and welcome to what we call the lifestyle of the peaceful and the patient.

Our experience in pursuing this process has taught us that there are a few milestones that most people experience as a result of making this new beginning. We offer these comments as a way to verify and confirm that this has happened to others and how it works out, but also to relate it to other spiritual paths and practices.

Many people come to this experience during a great reversal or breakdown in their lives – possibly health and healing issues, broken relationships or job losses – which are so overwhelming that they cannot see a way to understand why it has all happened and what to do. We call this the breakdown phase and advise that although it is the beginning of something wonderful, it is also very difficult. We want you to seek the best, most loving help that you can find and take very good care of yourself. And while you are taking really good care of yourself, take time to do nothing and just listen to your Higher Mind. Ask questions and keep a journal. It is very important to avoid fear and anxiety, as there is enough of that already. So make yourself as comfortable as possible and don't listen to anything that sounds discouraging or negative.

This is the time to rest and reflect, and so we call it the "do nothing" phase, which can last a long time. During this time, you have the opportunity to open up to redesigning your life and health based on a much higher view of reality. This is where the patience comes in. Do not expect results yet, as they will take time to appear, just stay peaceful and listen for positive guidance. If you have regrets, feelings of grief and guilt, accept them as having some good use and then let them go, as they have served their purpose and you are free to move on. Look at your life as an unfolding process, not as a finished product to be judged. We find that reciting positive affirmations is very helpful. Our favorites are: "What is the good in this experience?" "All good things come to me quickly and easily." "Everything will be all right." "I will find a way that is easy and good to a better life."

Do something every day that you like and enjoy, such as a walk or reading an inspirational book or just looking out of a window. Listen to only peaceful music or inspiring songs. Nature is a wonderful way to heal, as is creative expression.

Gradually, thoughts that are fearful come under control. And as you pay attention to more positive thoughts, they start to manifest better things in your life. Express gratitude, and remind yourself of the growing good in your life often – for they are confirmation that it is working for you to the good. Keep in mind that your soul is not punishing you or judging you. Many difficult experiences were chosen for a good outcome that was desired; so, do not judge yourself or anyone else.

Keep your heart open to loving yourself and say good things about yourself when you look in the mirror or talk to others. In not judging others, you do not need to forgive them. For they, in your mind, did not intend to harm you; they were prisoners of their own fears. Just avoid people who create harm, and send them love from a distance. If you find someone who needs help and does not intend to harm you, do give help that you can afford to do, as it energizes your self-esteem and participates in the giving and receiving of love that constitutes the Source of all Good. Never do harm to yourself or to anyone else, as it only brings harm back in greater quantities. Stay as peaceful as you can, and rest a lot. Such times require lots of rest, clean water, wholesome food and loving company.

Following the do nothing period, things get a lot better. And there is often an awareness of a desire to give service to others as a part of your life. Let that impulse be guided in a peaceful way. It should never involve self-sacrifice, abuse or deprivation. True service will bring you more benefits than you gave, but giving with the Intention for the Highest Good is the start of it all.

From then on, there will be a never-ending series of experiences, each better than before, leading you to realize the loving being that you are. Just being yourself will help the rest of us to be better, and the society as a whole will begin to get more wholesome and productive. There is no great cause or campaign to join. Opening to your Higher Mind is an unfolding of the Divine Plan of giving and receiving love in every moment and place.

For many, it is a much less dramatic experience, and their lives take a subtle turn for the better. They turn to favorite healthful practices and activities that enhance them in body, mind, emotion and spirit such as meditation, yoga, or exercise. Some meet a great teacher or read an inspiring book, and they find a sense of direction. Again, there is the call to serve others in some capacity that is easy and fulfilling.

For some, there is a strange experience such as hearing sounds that aren't there, impressive dreams or visions. Do not be afraid of these, but also do not focus on them. They are incidentals along the way. Our minds and bodies are very sensitive to changes in energy and produce some unusual occurrences. If you have concerns, seek competent help.

Lastly, I'd like to talk about grief relief. This is a natural process of a mind and body wishing to live in peace and not in fear. It is a fact of life on Earth that living in fear is very fearful, and the body reacts to fear by holding onto toxic substances, tensions, and distortions of its normal functions. In short, fear propels the body into disease. Once you decide to leave fear behind, all of these conditions will start to heal and abate. Some are so small a healing as sneezing several times, or slight diarrhea, a slight rise in temperature, a cold, or even stomach upset. The mild situations pass quickly, but a few of them may require professional help. Do not feel that you are alone. There are compassionate physicians, nurses, counseling therapists, chiropractors, and massage therapists who can help you to readjust. By slowly and gently releasing the toxins of fear, you are creating a healthy and happy life for yourself.

Our experience is that there is no need for speed, so take it slowly and patiently and let your body shed its weight of grief slowly and easily. Think of this time as a healing retreat. If you get into being fearful, go back to rest and reducing your activities. Again, lots of water, rest, and mild exercise of your choosing works very well. Consult help if you have any concerns that you cannot handle. The end result is health and rejuvenation of your energy and ability to function.

Additional Readings

The following section includes readings that I did on various topics about which that I wanted to inquire. I set the Intention for the Highest Good, asked a question and wrote down what I got. They will reflect my own abilities, interests, and experiences, so there will be some references to me and my situations. I do not offer them as absolute truth, just the best truth that I was able to access at the time. However, they are indeed very interesting and helpful, so I offer them to you for your help and to see that you can do these as well.

Keep in mind that everyone's experience is different, and it is possible that instead of words, you might get music or song, images, memories, sensations in your body or just a sense of knowing rather than words. I recommend that you just accept whatever you get without judgment and keep practicing. Thank yourself for what you got, but ask for better next time. Relax, and don't try too hard. It is actually much easier than you are expecting. And, in fact, you have been doing it all of your life, you just didn't recognize it for what it was.

If you get anything scary, critical or stressful, stop and ask again later when you are more peaceful and positive because negative experiences are an indication that you are getting Conscious Mind ego, assumptions, and fears. Do not ask for a reading when you are hungry, tired or uncomfortable. Also, being in a quiet, natural, peaceful, and comfortable place is very helpful. If you are on mind-altering drugs, or have a mental or emotional illness, I recommend that you not attempt this and seek professional help as soon as possible as you may not be able to overcome the difficulties without help. As an alternative, ask a friend or family member to pray for your health and well being while you seek help.

As you are reading these articles, there will be strange wordings, redundant sentence structure, and other anomalies of translation of spirit thoughts to the digital page. I've done my best to edit them, but feel free to ask your own Higher Mind for further explanation or contact us with a question. Some people form small groups to study their own readings on certain topics, and we find that it can be very helpful if everyone agrees to cooperate in keeping ego and fear out of the discussions. Always set the Intention for the Highest Good and nothing else. So, here goes. Enjoy, and let us know what you think.

Forgiveness and Enlightenment: An Introduction

Peace and Light Association
Peaceandlight01@aol.com
PeaceandLight.net
Copyright: 2013

Forgiveness is the essential step in the enlightenment process that causes the Conscious Mind to come into cooperation with the guidance of the Higher Mind. By taking a step back into the past, the Conscious Mind brings up many experiences that seem to be of harm or hurt and posits the phrase: "See, I told you so. This life of yours is a dangerous place to be. You could get hurt here. Better protect yourself." Again the evidence of events and society's consensual understanding of what life is about comes to the forefront for the protection of the ego's right to make it's own interpretations.

Once the seeker decides to listen to both minds and to repair the lesser with the healing gifts of the greater, the path to enlightenment has started. And so, it begins something like this:

Joyce: Why did this happen to me? What was wrong with me or what was wrong with the other who hurt me? But before I receive an answer, I request that it lead to more happiness not less, for I have learned that to merely review the past in misery causes it to proliferate.

Peaceful One: As you ask for good, then so it will be, so let's see what really happened. Did not the other seem to be mean and selfish, a true sign of one in fear? Did not that other one give you a taste of what he or she was feeling by attempting to hurt you as well or worse than he or she had been hurt?

Joyce: OK, I'm willing to see that. So how does that help?

Peaceful One: If I am in fear and give my fear to you, and you take it and turn it into peace, then I have truly lost the fear for the moment and you have never really received it.

Joyce: That's sounds like the right thing to do, but it's not what I did. I took it as fear. I got very angry and hurt for a long time. Indeed, it triggered my own deepest fears as well. I feared that I could be rejected, hurt and left to be alone with no one to love and support me.

Peaceful One: Indeed, you did, but where did you turn to find true love and true support?

Joyce: To you, of course, for there was no one else there, and you did such a good job of it.

Peaceful One: Well, then the Highest Good was indeed given and received. For you left in peace and found the Highest Good, and the other left in peace and had the opportunity to find another path to peace. If one does not choose the easy way of peacefulness, each always has the option to recycle over and over in pain until one tires of it and chooses another path such as you have done. So our estimation is that much good has been done and little if any harm done.

Joyce: So how should I look at such people and the experience?

Peaceful One: As the best that could have been had. Gratitude for the enlightenment is an appropriate response. In addition, wishing this one, from afar, to be given the best path to the same enlightenment would be delightful as well, for it would make you a great giver. And thus, your self-esteem would be rich with the experience.

Joyce: What about all of the things and money that others unfairly took from me? Is it an eye for an eye and I get it all back somehow, like the Bible says?

Peaceful One: That Bible quote was a teaching that no one is less than another: that all eyes are the same, so one cannot justify taking another's.

However, to answer your questions about the goods of the household being divided unfairly, that is the matter of divorce courts to decide, for nothing that you lost was of the value of what you retained, for the deeds of each day are determined by the intention of the doers. And the doer with the intention of the Highest Good always rests supreme, for it implies that all will receive what they need. And thus, it was. Others got what they needed to move on and not be a disturbance to your peace, and you got what you needed to simplify and clean up your home so your peacefulness could thrive. Your prompt return to work is a clear demonstration that abundance began to flow to you at exactly the right time and will never cease to exist as long as you intend for the Highest Good to be your lot in life.

Joyce: OK, so everything turned out perfectly, giving me a much better life?

Peaceful One: Yes, and a much better life is defined as the path to enlightenment. So let's proceed with a new reading on the nature of forgiveness and enlightenment.

Forgiveness and Enlightenment, 3.7.11

Association for Peace and Light
Inquire at: peaceandlight01@aol.com
PeaceandLight.net

Once the great barrier between physical life and spirit life has been broached and the awesome prospect of learning all that the universe has to offer is at one's doorstep, one is immediately aware that there is someone else, very needy, still tugging at one's coat tails, so to speak. At once thought of as a small mind, the Conscious Mind is actually more like a frightened child in need of nurturing, care, education, and attentive guidance. Until that child has been made to be happy, nothing else can proceed. So the doorway to grace will, at first, have to be used mainly for healing the Conscious Mind. For the first law is to heal what needs healing the most. And until all are healed, no one can advance. So once again, the voice of the Conscious Mind is given the blessing of the attention of the Higher Mind.

With the prospect that one could possibly be a Being of Light, there is only the fact of the filters to be removed to have it shining bright and beautiful. For the light is the light, and it is never diminished except in the mind of the beholder. Therefore, that mind must take the courage to look directly at the light and find itself to be one with it. In simple terms, that is the enlightenment process that is required of the seeker. And so forgiveness is that process of letting the scales fall from one's eyes so that the light can be seen. And, in finding forgiveness to be yet another form of enlightenment, as this one wishes to give to others, we invite her to share her own experience of the forgiveness process through the asking and answering of questions.

Q. What is the definition of grief?

A. Grief is the need to hold the sleight of hand called hurt tightly to the consciousness, heart and body. The soul knows that no hurt has occurred, thus it rejects the whole concept and proceeds on the path to joy and happiness. But the Conscious Mind is sure that it is really hurt and even implants the knowledge in the body, where it can cause illness and discomfort. When the stretching between the beliefs of the two minds is so severe that it is painful, then a decision must be made. For the outcomes will become more severe between the nature of the Higher Mind to race to peace and the desire of the Conscious Mind to hold onto pain and misery and eventually death. Usually the position of the Conscious Mind becomes completely untenable, and so the painful process of releasing grief begins.

In stating the need to avoid speeding on a collision course to bodily pain, to be entirely alone during this process is the right way to engage in this process. And we urge others to do the same. For it is in the personal recall of all the hurts, slings, and arrows – imagined by the Conscious Mind to be of real importance – that the Conscious Mind regains its self-esteem. And it is in self-esteem that it can continue to relinquish its death hold upon the heart and body of the griever.

Q. What do you mean imagined hurts?

A. The Conscious Mind imagines that the intentions of another's Conscious Mind can impact its awareness in some profound way. Actually, the so-called hurt is none other than the conflict of the Conscious Mind seeking its own way and being thwarted by the will of another. And in finding that none but the will of the Higher Mind can be trusted, the Conscious Mind loses ground in the painful delusion of separation, for it sought to control the entity called another for its own preservation.

Thus, in finding that there is no way that anyone can truly be hurt by another, the Conscious Mind, which assumes that it is separate and alone, loses all hope of ever demeaning the Being of Light with the self-concept of demise. And in lacking the ability to control the Body of Light, the Conscious Mind never needs to be in demise again – for it is intimately a part of the Soul. The true defeat is the thought of separation. For as one loves and cares for the other, the truth of the common existence comes to be seen for what it truly is, a Great Oneness loving all parts of itself.

 The experience of grief relief is a powerful one. When the Conscious Mind enlightens itself to the forecast that none but the best of events will occur to its awareness in the future, it loosens its hold on the ability to ever again torment the mind, body and, soul or to ever again be reborn into yet another lifetime of greed for pain and misery. For Enlightened Ones have entered into yet another contract than the average person seeking redress from an individual painful event seeks to do. The Enlightened One needs nothing less than the full enlightenment of the process of being impervious to all that is less than peace and happiness forever.

It is for this reason that we have sent this little one to be a reader, as she has achieved her enlightenment and once more is enlightening the other members of the family with her innocent comment on the day that her life changed: "It's time for you to leave, for I desire to be in peace and only peace." If she had not done so, she might have been convinced that the lack of a kind word or deed from another would make her feel rejected and unloved. However, being recovered into peace consciousness, she rejoices in being alive and able to see and feel the bright light of another day.

Q. How does the peace consciousness play into this process?

A. The peace consciousness plays the same song that the pied piper played: "Play with me, and I will lead you to happiness and contentment." For the peaceful ways of one displayed to the others demonstrate that the need for speed to be judgmental and rejecting have been unproductive of the fruits of peace. So, therefore, the proper process for an Enlightened One to use in any situation of conflict is to withdraw into peace and to rest for a day or two, recovering the prize of peace. Later, the peaceful consequences of those days and nights of peace consciousness bring the removal of fear and greed in the minds of others as well. And thus, all are provided quite a nice repair of the attitudes toward the peaceful ways.

It was for this reason that Jesus frequently went away to be alone. It was for the repair of His own peace consciousness and for the lacking of His presence to be made to be felt by the others so that their awareness could be raised. And being raised over and over again, they gained their own awareness about needing their own aloneness to protect it themselves. For in protecting peace, we mean to allow the body, mind and heart time to adjust at all levels to the proper measure of peace that can be allowed to those whose only desire is for peace.

It is the gift of the Higher Mind to command the peace consciousness, but the heart, Conscious Mind and body need time lags to adjust or its consciousness will be duly disturbed with an illness or unrest of some kind. Thus, there is the need for retreats of many kinds.

Q. Why do we retreat to places of nature rather than to the cities and inhabited areas?

A. Why not process the peace of enlightenment where the enlightenment is in its most rich form? The forming of peace consciousness is indeed a productive process in which those who possess nothing of conflict will proceed to give peace to those who seek it. It is for this reason that a farm is the perfect place for this to occur. For in being peacefulness itself, a farm has many plants, animals and natural scenes. Also it lacks the interference of many other layers of Conscious Mind in less natural areas. The mind, heart and body have the opportunity to relax and resist peace no longer. Because the farm has been given over to the peace process, it will remain intact for the use of the Mystery School, for the forgiveness given there will not ever be reversed.

For this reason, the class reunion of the old Mystery Schools has been initiated. These lasting experiences of peace inhibit the return to pain and misery in the lives of those investing in peace, for their true home is only a thought away. For it is in being a Body Of Light that they have come to remember for themselves the experiences of the Ancient Egyptian Mystery School classes, and the class on forgiveness is the first of many such classes.

Q. What is a Lost One?

A. One who is said to be a Lost One has found for him or herself that the way of peacefulness is not what it originally seemed to be. It required them to practice their own brand of restraint, self-care, and patience with themselves. Having no need for such as this, they hurried off to do their ego's own will, and in so doing have not made much progress and have injured themselves and potentially others by their negativity, rejection, and projection of their own needs onto others who have come to do nothing but to help them.

However, in performing one single deed of kindness to a lost one, the Enlightened Ones may come and then go on their way for their own comfort. For in days gone by and in some cultures, such a kindness might have been repaid by humiliation in the eyes of others or even loss of their lives on the Earth plane. Many have been called martyrs, but seek no more to be such as these. For the times have grown dim of such acts of one upon the other, and, finally, the Earthly societies have mostly outlawed such acts. Thus it is possible in times of peace for the Lost Ones and Enlightened Ones to befriend, birth or marry each other and have no need to be parted until one attempts to destroy the peace of the other.

When such a bond is broken, it is because the Peaceful One insists on peace and the Unpeaceful One flees with the consequences of the need for speed following close upon their heels. Thus, it is found that many upon the Earth plane have had divorces and disagreements, but yet have come and gone in much more peace. These are the days of approaching world-wide peace.

If one shall offer peace once again to the other, then the opportunity is available for the Unpeaceful One to return in this or another life for the purpose of acceptance of peace, and perhaps one shall teach the other. For in finding the repentance of even one of these lost sheep, the shepherd rejoices just as if all the others had returned as well. For the Highest Good requires: As one progresses on the peaceful path, the others do so as well.

Amen, we say to you, that no act or deed of kindness is ever reversed upon the Higher Plane. Only the lower plane could see any event as anything but the work of the Highest Good. And so it is with gladness that we send the message that where peacekeepers dare to tread is where there is nothing ever again to dread.

Q. Thank you for this reading. How should it be used?

A. By answering your questions, you have questions no more. And in being satisfied, you have taken the great wisdom and made it your own possession. And as you continue through your lives, you will remember to turn once and again inward to where the kingdom of heaven resides. Amen.

Commentary

In this reading, there is reference to the ancient Mystery Schools, the most famous and well documented was established in ancient Egypt before 10,00 BC. Many who attended these schools in past lives have returned in this life to promote the path to peace. They were once students and teachers in these schools, and so they come with great interest and remember much of what was taught. You might be one of them. If so, your entrance into Higher Mind will feel like coming home, and you will indeed know that you know the way. You may already know what your path of service is and how to access your Higher Mind to get assistance.

However, in the reading, I once again considered how the Conscious Mind views things versus the Higher Mind. I found a new view of how the others in my life who have been both givers of grief as well as grace work for the Highest Good. Grace, being the gift of the Highest Good as it shows up in life by means of the easy way, I wondered how it works. Remembering that I could never really be hurt once I had dedicated my life to the Highest Good gave me confidence to see others in a new light.

Brothers and Sisters of Grace, 9.29.12

Peace and Light Association
Peaceandlight01@aol.com
PeaceandLight.net
Copyright 2012

We would like to comment on the need for grace as opposed to the need for speed. Should one see the other side of life as being the place from which grace flows, then there may be the need to be in a lack on your side and an abundance on our side. And thus, we are separate, but can cooperate. However, if we see ourselves as one being of strength with all of the grace of the universe at our disposal, then there is the need to be seen as merely the applicator of grace from one to the other for the pleasure of doing so. Much like one partner rubs the back of the other to create comfort and then is given much the same in return.

Thus, we would like to inform you that you have given us your name to speak as a doer of the Highest Good, and so we have arranged the events of every moment to be given as a graceful and beautiful experience and never harmful. With this in mind, there is never the need to be in alarm, untidy, hurried, or unsafe in any way. For we merely see the need for some grace before each moment of your life occurs and apply it well in advance. Therefore, all that is needed from you is to just apply the grace in reverse by being grateful.

And as a grace reversal soul of your own kind, you have your nature to consider. Do not hesitate to give grace to another who reacts in fear, for you are protected. You are free to pray for their Highest Good and never say a word or to give a small kindness and then disappear. You do not need to accomplish much on the physical plane for them to succeed. You can confidently turn them over to the Highest Good and rest in peace and we will show up for miracles to be performed. For when you give grace to one of these, even the smallest one, you engage the heavenly hosts and ultimately do it unto God.

And so, although all may seem to be separate entities for the moment, there is yet another grain of truth to be added to the long story. For from one parent may come many children, but they are all loved and nourished by the parent in much the same way as an animal might carry its young wherever it goes only to deposit them in places where they can grow and prosper when the time in right.

And so one must assume that once the nature of the one Source has been analyzed, that it, being a parent of wise choice, has issued the desire to be one with all of it's offspring. And so it must be said that one is the same as the other in being loved, if not the same in face or form or figure. With that said, there are some who would come and make faces that are scary. And none but the wisest would ever be able to see within that one the grace that is carried and the love that is given from within. However, it is so.

Once the commitment is made to be able to see each other as offspring of a single parent and thus siblings of nature, there is the question of why and how siblings fight and squabble. Is it not to acquire an over supply of some resource, whether it be the attention of the parent, a toy, or food or even freedom to play alone?

And of necessity, we come back once again to the nature of the Conscious Mind to misunderstand as any child would do, until it learns better than to be jealous of one another and learn to share and not to be at war with one another. For in all things, there is a reason and a season, as the old text would say. And the reason is to be in grace at all times and places and the season is now. For in portraying oneself to be at one with God, then we must share His desire to raise his children in grace and to share all that is necessary for their raising and nurturing.

And with this, we leave you with the thought that never is there a need for forgiveness if it is merely my brother or sister who has sinned, for he is my brother and she is my sister. With that being said, there are way too many ways in which to help each other, that we cannot even count them. And so we love to traverse each day with the accomplishment of at least one thing to make it easier for a sibling to progress in the right direction and not the wrong. And if you do the same, you will do grace.

For how could right or wrong be judged in any other way than this? There is no need in heaven or Earth greater than that to be at-one with the Source and each other. For the long journey has no end, even though there is great grace in the giving and receiving of grace at this momentous point in time. With that, we bid you adieu and say "Amen," although it is more properly termed: All men and women are mine, and I love them all and appreciate your help in getting them back to my embrace.

About the Peace and Light Association

After you have read the conversations part of this book, I guess you know why we chose these two words as the name of our association. But to reiterate, peace is the way into the Higher Mind, and then your Light becomes free of fear and the manifestations of your life change for the better. Everything else is Highest Good of all kinds and descriptions, all unique to you and your needs.

A few of my friends and I formed this small association, which is an educational organization to offer to the world what we have discovered. We do not have any religious or philosophical affiliations nor challenge any beliefs that others may have. We offer what we have learned and leave it up to you, the reader, to judge for yourself what is right for you. It is our belief and practice that each person has the ability to access their own Higher Mind and can enjoy complete Higher Guidance on virtually any topic. Since that guidance comes from a good Source, the results are always good and never in conflict or cause harm. No one needs to control another. Each is totally capable of reaching his or her highest potential using the resources within themselves.

The Highest Good requires that there be no harm and lots of good, and we follow that principle. We have found that those who live under the guidance of their Higher Minds live peaceful, patient, healthy and loving lives of service to others, so they make good friends and citizens. You can expect the same for your life.

We have a website and an e-mail address for inquiries regarding future books, classes, conferences, retreats, news. and talks that we offer.

Your access to your Higher Mind is your inalienable birthright, and no one can keep you from it – nor do you need anyone to give it to you. Neither does anyone know any more than you or have any status more or less than you. We offer the classes only as a convenience and to enjoy the company of others doing the same thing. We believe that your destiny is to be a fully independent channel of your own Higher Mind through a warm and loving heart and to do what is the Highest Good within the context of your life path. For that reason, we do not do personal readings for individuals, as everyone is fully capable of doing their own in the privacy of their own heart. Our work is to encourage that heart to be peaceful enough so that the channel can be accurately heard.

In addition, from time to time, there will be on the website, new topic readings on various subjects as well as a Contact Us option for your comments. Our commitment to you is to channel our Higher Minds for the Highest Good and nothing else.

PeaceandLight.net
peaceandlight01@aol.com

Recommended Books and DVDs

You Can Heal Your Life by Louise Hay. This book gives empowering affirmations that are effective in turning away from fear and moving to the Highest Good.

There Is A River by Thomas Sugrue. This is about the life and philosophy of Edgar Cayce. Once you read this book, there are thousands more about his life and work on the **edgarcayce.org** website.

Edgar Cayce on Channeling Your Higher Self by Henry Reed. This book is as close as I've found to interpreting what Cayce said about contacting Higher Mind.

The Power of Now by Eckhart Tolle. This book describes one person's beginning experience. It is a good description of the difference between the Conscious Mind and the Higher Mind.

Broken Open by Elizabeth Lesser. This book talks about the process of using difficult situations in life for the good.

Supervisor's Training Guide: The How-To Book for New and Experienced Supervisors by Joyce Karnes. This is a book that I wrote to teach supervisors and managers how to use the Highest Good at work.

Set of DVD's: *The Pyramid Code* by Dr. Carmen Boulter, PHD. (www.kultur.com) The team that made these DVD's were, in my opinion, using their Higher Minds. They offer a very different way of interpreting The Golden Age of Egypt. I think that anyone interested in Egyptology, would get a good introduction to these monuments and artifacts.

Recommended Websites

PeaceandLight.net

This is our association website, and we offer information on the path to peace, links to other good sites and schedules for classes and conferences. You can purchase a copy of this and future books on Amazon.com in Kindle or softbound form. We will announce future books on the site.

As we find other Mystery School returnees who have set upon the path to peace, we will offer links to their works as well. In fact, soon, we will be pleased to offer music that has been specifically channeled for healing through the five steps. This music was developed by a returnee who remembered his talents and skills.

We would be happy to conduct "Reading Classes" to help others to open to their Higher Mind. Also, we would be glad to initiate small groups who have a specific project or topic what they wish to research through their Higher Minds.

EdgarCayce.org

This is the official website of the Association for Research and Enlightenment, representing the foundation that Edgar Cayce left behind after his death. It houses the library of his readings as well as many other good books and resources. The association has an active lecture and conference schedule, and we teach there often. The center is a beautiful place full of peace, and we highly recommend the meditation garden, library, bookstore, and meditation room on the top floor.

HayHouse.com

This is the site for the organization that Louise Hay founded. Her landmark book, *You Can Heal your Life,* has propelled millions on the same path that I am describing here. The organization has conferences, books, an Internet radio program, and is generally a great resource for people living the lifestyle of the peaceful and patient.

avisionintoyou.com

This is the site of Jim Herman who is a Medical Intuitive. He has learned from Higher Mind how to help people heal themselves through asking the Great Oneness to send them healings. He essentially lends his strength of will to that of the petitioner, forming a strong opening for grace. His work is dedicated to the Highest Good, and so thus it is. He gives classes and has individual appointments over the phone or in person to conduct this process.

Peacepiper.net

This is the site for Phil Crabtree who has remembered how to heal through the playing of music. He can channel your unique song and play the tones for the healing of each part of the body. Edgar Cayce said that such healing was common in ancient Egypt in the Temple Beautiful. Phil has recreated it for us now.

Stephanievanhoose.com

Stephanie is a spiritual medium and reader who started her own radio show to introduce the general public to the use of the Higher Mind. Her website has many good links and stories, and you can schedule a personal reading. Look for her radio show which is available by Internet and listen for the many good topics that she brings to her show.

The Oneness University

This organization started in India and has spread around the world. It teaches how to release grief and to experience the Blessing of Oneness. It provides a lot of support and a social circle of awakened ones. You can get more information and a link at Jim's site: avisionintoyou.com

About Our Cover and Logo

On the cover is the peaceful, sunny view of the farm that inspired this book. With much to be grateful for, I have dedicated this land and home to the peaceful energy of the Christ Consciousness which has been growing and expanding for several years. As it does, there are many miracles of open minds and hearts that occur here.

Also on our logo is the image of the ankh, which was the symbol for the Highest Good in ancient Egypt. It is the form of a person whose arms are open to receive the Presence of God and whose mind is open to Higher Mind. Most ankhs have a single stand representing the determination to stand firm with the desire to remove fear and to pursue the Highest Good, but our ankh has the walking legs that symbolize the desire to carry the Highest Good to all corners of the Earth and give away its many gifts and healings as we walk through life.

The ankh, the symbol of Highest Good, is placed on the image of the Earth because the Earth is now poised to be healed of Conscious Mind fears and to be wrapped in the golden light. This is the meaning of the end of the Mayan calendar. It recorded the end of the years of the rule of the Conscious Mind. Many Great Ones have arrived to write the next chapter in peace and in light. The gold lines on the Earth represent the interconnecting ley lines used as sites of pyramids and temples, which will be recharged and reused for raising the energy of the Earth for peace. They will also be used again to charge our bodies of light with the Highest Good. It also represents the use of the Internet to freely and rapidly disseminate useful information to all so that all will have the information as to how to live in peace. The color purple represents grief relief, and blue is healing.

Our slogan is: "Open to the Highest Good and Live in Peace and Light." In order to open to Higher Mind, the state of peace is necessary and if you stick with it long enough, following its guidance, it gives you so much light energy that you heal and rejuvenate. It is truly a simple, but grand way to live. The plus or ampersand sign indicates that we work together in small groups, giving and receiving help and love and can yield much more than one could by working alone.

In many Egyptian tombs, the ceilings are painted with a blue background with gold stars touching each other. When I asked the Peaceful One the meaning of the beautiful ceilings, I was told that the stars represented the Great Oneness that is just across the barrier between the two minds and rests eager and willing to help and guide us living on Earth. All of the stars or souls are touching, so they know and help each other. It is like a great network or fabric. I thought that it would make a good design for our efforts.

+

We plan to be a conduit of information and grace which will spark each person who is ready and interested to open to his or her own Higher Mind and to start their own process of healing and guidance. Each has their own path and plan and should answer only to the Highest Good, which gives nothing but good and never any harm. Thus we can all live in freedom, but also constantly grow in grace, while giving and receiving good in many different ways.

One path might consist of being a parent in love with parenting many who come into this existence. Others might be managers of companies or engineers or workers in kitchens who cook with attention and grace so all can be nourished. Some might be well meaning connoisseurs of all paths, skipping merrily from the giving of one kind of grace to another. As well, a dog walker, government official, or a social worker appears at their work with grace in their heart and attention to the workings of love on their minds. They all bless their work with the intention to be at peace themselves and to give the Highest Good at all times and nothing else. They address any interaction as coming from a beloved one and going to a beloved one who is in need.

Nothing else is required for all that works in grace has grace to depend upon and no need will go begging or want to be lacking for either the giver or the receiver. In fact the greatest giver will be the most prosperous and healthy of all for that one will be possessed of a great need of the resources to serve those with the least. No one will be harmed, for they have all of their needs addressed and their proper name to be called and thus they turn into blessed ones themselves in need of a service to provide to another in need.

Thus all will be raised and made whole and attention can be raised to the situation of the restoration of the Earth's peaceful atmosphere, water, and resources without anyone giving up anything that they need. Once completed, the plan is to address the peace of the whole solar system.

For peace begets peace and war begets war, so let's give peace a chance this time and for all times, for the alternative is very sad. Although it may take a thousand years of peace building, there will be no harm and so much good that it will be astounding and thus the ancient promise will be fulfilled: "Go and multiply all manner of good and I will be by your side enjoying every moment with you and guiding you every step of the way."

Forward to the Next Book

The Book of the Highest Good, Volume Two: Walk to Freedom

After finishing this book and almost sending it off to be published, I had to add another moment of truth to share with you, Dear Reader. I had a series of significant dreams and, since I had started the habit of doing a typed daily dialogue with the Peaceful One, I asked about the dreams and was given a hint of what the next volume is to be about. I thought that maybe you would be interested and join me once again.

+

Joyce: Peaceful One, I've had dreams lately about people that I've known and then lost touch with. I meet them again in the dream and they are so different than what I remembered they were. Some of them did not treat me very well. I feel that you are talking to me about relationships in general. What are you trying to teach me?

Peaceful One: How would I ever know unless you had trusted me to be your guide in this great matter of your heart? Do you realize that once you close your mind to another and say that one is for fear and the other for peace, there will be no other in your life? For one is the flip side of the other. Maybe these people are coming to you for a purpose that is good.

Joyce: Interesting. Why are they coming to me now?

157

Peaceful One: Soon there will be one, then the other. For how could you have come to this work without the great friends who helped you and accompanied you before?

Joyce: So these are old friends and coworkers. Well I would be glad to have them back, even if we have a lot to catch up with and maybe some forgiveness to share. By the way, what are we supposed to be doing together?

Peaceful One: Should one show up and tell you just the same as I, then you will know how to behave. These are the Mystery School attendees who have pledged themselves to be at one with you in the starting of the first century of peace of these times. How would that be for you to be surrounded by those who came from so long ago just to be of assistance?

Joyce: I'd be so happy.

Peaceful One: Well, then, we must put out some bait so to speak for them to recognize who it is who addresses them. From far and wide they will come to be in your classes and to attend your retreats. And when they leave, they will have remembered themselves and have made an even better contribution to the peace project than was done before.

Joyce: That sounds wonderful. What do we have to do?

Peaceful One: First let's try being of grace and taking a rest from this keyboard and then while walking down the lane think about the long walk to freedom from fear that you have initiated. Would that sound like a good title for the next book?

Joyce: I would be pretty excited about that, wouldn't you? OK, I guess that is the beginning of the second book. It sounds like I would be describing more about how the refusal to be fearful has felt for me and how it has played out in my life. That would remind Dear Readers about their own experiences and maybe bring them to their own recollections of how they did it long ago. By the way, were we all together in ancient Egypt?

Peaceful One: More or less, but then less the location than it was the intention for the old schools were far flung over the Earth and many who left to established more elsewhere, never to return in that lifetime, thus there is a yearning for all to start once again at a home location and then to take it all over the world once again. You were all such friends and family. Your relationships were all about intending good for each other and making the gifts of the Higher Mind available for each other. In fact, you founded many a society on just such a turn of events. Without the influence of the Higher Mind and the Highest Good, relationships are full of difficulties, disappointments and disasters of all kinds.

Joyce: Tell me about it.

Peaceful One: Well, that will be the topic of the next book. How can relationships of all kinds be opportunities for one being to channel God to another and vice versa without causing harm? A pretty good topic, don't you think?

Joyce: Yes, I think so. If we could solve that problem, then we'd probably be more open to others regardless of their state of fear and peace. Thank you for opening up this topic. I see that you are once again leading me in a very kind, gentle and wise way into healing myself so that I can own happiness and then give it away. And thank you for calling back together the lost family. I've been lonely without them.

Peaceful One: I couldn't have done it without you. They have been yearning to be with you as well. Such a family is a blessing to each other and to the Earth. And with that, so many others will be healed as well for you are never content with hiding great secrets. You are a healer of yourself and the world as best you can do. We salute you, support you and enlighten you. As you progress on this path, there are so many more who wish to sit in this seat and to find within themselves the same loving wisdom that does not disappoint or harm. And so at once the beginning has been made, but never an ending. Rest now for you have much to do to prepare for Volume Two.

The Calling Together

Dedication: We have not but a moment in time to tell our stories, be they stories of crime and defeat or victories of the heart. But nowhere in time do we find that those whose best times were those spent together will ever be apart for long. They always know how to find each other at just the right times and places. So for these, we write these words as a calling to the Mystery School Returnees to come once again to be together in peace. We call them to teach and to portray in their lives once more how a society formed in the intention for the Highest Good can prosper in peace.

Companions on the Path of Peace

Moments in time speed by like comets in the sky.
I've been missing your company so long, making loneliness a dire retreat.
I've been missing the joinings and gatherings found only in my memories.
Where have you been, knowing now is the time for darkness to retreat?

So much must be said to make time spend its hope, so release the grief.
Lest we forget, time meant no harm, so bring no regrets.
Oh, I know that a promise given but not remembered is costly indeed.
But please forgive the false promises and the failings of all.

For if we are to have time honored as our friend, we must see more.
For those whose passages can only be marked with "I'm sorry,"
Time could be a road to perdition, but we forbad something so sad.
We know forgiveness is a sure voyage of joining again. We can all be safe.

So, don't let grief make meeting again a dangerous thing.
We've all lost and then gained and walked on in the rain.

Knowing that the best of friends would recognize each other
Throughout the bloom and the gloom of so many lives in time.

Rejoice that time has brought friends together at last,
So we can gather in celebration to join and outlast the repast.
For this, we once said our vows, making our greatest promises to be true.
And coming together is so sweet and we will not to be denied its bliss.

To find home, you will have to listen to the calling of the angelic realms,
For they know who we are, where we reside and when we are to meet.
They make merry the welcome and hasten the departure of defeats.
They consider all giving and receiving to be of peace. We did not err.

As we meet, we will exchange the secret sign of heaven's goodness
spent,
Both offered and accepted without any reservations.
Hesitant at first, but solidly content, the parties of friends want no
retreat,
From the company of companions on the path they call peace.

We will care for each others' wounds and offer our peace,
Profoundly relieved to be once again in such good care.
And none but the laughter of happy refrains would we give.
For we are the company of companions on the path they call peace.

In the name of the Highest Good, welcome home.

9/9/10